The Distiller's Guide to Rum

White Mule Press, Hayward, CA 94541
© 2013 by White Mule Press
Printed in the United States of America

ISBN-13: 978-0-9910436-0-6

THE DISTILLER'S GUIDE TO RUM

by

Ian Smiley, Eric Watson
& Michael Delevante

With Contributions by
Eric Zandona and Martin Cate

published by
White Mule Press
Hayward, CA

Table of Contents

x Foreword

xii Introduction

Part One

Historic and Contemporary Rum Producers

5 The Story of Rum

13 On Site with New England Distilleries

Part Two

How to Make Rum

37 Equipment

41 Raw Ingredients

53 Molasses Pretreatment

57 Fermentation

67 Distillation

73 Batch Distillation of Rum Utilizing a Rectification Column

81 Maturation, Blending & Vatting

85 Example Recipe for Amber Rum

Part Three

Rum Resources

95 Rum Styles

101 Reinventing Classic Rum Cocktails

105 Best Rum Bars in the World

109 Rum Festivals

111 Bibliography of Rum

117 Rum On-line

Appendix

123 Fundamentals of Distillation

137 Glossary

144 Index

Foreword

A new American Revolution in Rum has started. From Hawaii to
New England, craft distillers across the United States have begun to
reassert rum's place as an American spirit beyond the confines of the
Caribbean and Latin America. In 2003, rum made up about 12% of the
total volume of spirits consumed in the United States and has continued
to slowly grow in market share with most of the growth in the high-end
premium and super premium bottlings.[1] For those distillers interested
in entering the rum market, now is the time to do so and this book can
help you do it. *The Distiller's Guide to Rum* contains the accumulated
knowledge of three of the world's experts on the topic of rum distillation.

Michael Delevante was born and raised in Jamaica, and is the Senior
Distiller for Appleton Estate Jamaican Rum. After earning a degree
in Chemical Engineering, Michael started working at the Appleton
Distillery as a supervisor and then Distillery Manager. During his tenure
he has overseen the distillation of all their rums and he even redesigned
their distillation systems. Besides working for Appleton he has honed
his skill working with McGuinness Distillers and Wray & Nephew
Distilleries. In 1992, Delevante set up a specialized beverage consulting
company in Canada called Delevante & Associates. Michael has been
known to give informative talks and seminars on the topic of rum which
has earned him the nick name, the "Rum Doctor."[2]

Ian Smiley is the author of the book, *Making Pure Corn Whiskey*, an
Amphora Society publication, which is currently in its third edition.
He has written articles for a number of magazines such as *The American
Distiller*, and he is the owner of Smiley's Home Distilling, an e-store
dedicated to home and laboratory distillers.[3] He frequently consults
on the start-up of small artisan distilleries, and is currently part owner
of a whisky distillery in China, L.S. Moonshine LLC, and Dover
Enterprises Distilleries in Simcoe, Ontario. As a distillery consultant,
Ian has designed the distilling operation for Last Mountain Distillery

1 International Wine Center, "The US Spirits Market," October 2004. Accessed January 7 2013,
http://www.internationalwinecenter.com/download/US%20Spirits%20Market.pdf; Distilled
Spirits Council of the United States, "Rum: If you like Pina Coladas...," February 2012. Accessed
January 7 2013, http://www.discus.org/assets/1/7/Rum2011.pdf. DISCUS defines High End
Premium as $130 to $175 supplier revenue/ 9 liters and Super Premium as anything over $175
supplier revenue/ 9 liters.

2 The UNU Institute for Water, Environment & Health, accessed November 20, 2012 http://
www.inweh.unu.edu/River/KnowledgeManagement/Kstar2012RumTasting.htm

3 Smiley's Home Distilling www.home-distilling.com

in Lumsden, Saskatchewan as well as formulating each of their whiskey and vodka products. Ian is currently doing the same for a number of other start-up distilleries.

Eric Watson spent twelve years of his work life as the corporate vice president of an industrial process contracting firm before he transitioned into the brewing industry. He opened Mesa Maltworks Microbiological in the early 1990's which specialized in yeast propagation and bacteriological audits for the brewing industry. However, as needs in the brewing industry shifted it led to the formation of AlBevCon LLC, a consultancy for the brewing and distilling industries.

In addition to his marketing degree, Watson graduated from the Siebel Institute of Technology with a diploma in brewing science and has received continuing education from Heriot-Watt University in Edinburgh, Scotland, the Technische Universitat Munchen Weihenstephan and Versuch- und Lehranstalt für Brauerei in Berlin. During his career, Watson has been the recipient of 16 professional brewing awards and 8 awards for distilled spirits. He serves as a judge for the US Brewer's Association at both the Great American Beer Festival and the World Beer Cup as well as judging for the BJCP. In addition to his involvement in the brewing industry, Watson is an author and educator for the American Distilling Institute, training members in the art and science of producing whisky, rum, vodka and other distilled spirits as well as facility design and operations management.

Eric Watson was instrumental in the establishment of the Cayman Island's first distillery, the Cayman Islands Spirits Company. There he assisted in the exploration and use of kinetic maturation which led to the development of the world's first underwater matured spirit, Seven Fathoms Rum. Since then he has helped design and establish distilleries in the US, Canada and the Caribbean, many of which have a rum focus.

—*Eric Zandona*

Introduction

This book was inspired by the recent popularity of rum among the cocktail circles, and by the advent of so many new rum distilleries in North America. Rum is now being made in micro-distilleries all over the United States, including a return to the original epicenter of rum distilling, Newport, Rhode Island. At the time of the American Revolution, there were about 30 rum distilleries in Rhode Island, 22 of which were in Newport alone, and the rum produced there was revered by some as the best in the world. The last Rhode Island rum distillery of that era closed in the 1840s. But, now they are coming back and not only in Rhode Island, but in all of New England, and across the United States and Canada.

In this book, you'll read about the story of rum and how it is made, written by the well-known distillery expert, Michael Delevante. The book also details the ingredients, equipment, and processes used to make rum. You will learn about the lubricious effects of barrel aging, and the various ways that it is done. And, there is a chapter that explains step-by-step how to make a 155-gallon batch of rum mash and how to distill and age it, written by Ian Smiley. This chapter gives a new micro-distillery a proven recipe and process to get a running start in producing their first product. There is also a chapter on the batch distillation of rum using a hybrid batch distillation system comprised of a pot still and a rectification column written by Eric Watson of AlBevCon LLC.

Ian Smiley visited three new rum distilleries in New England and conducted extensive interviews with the owners and their staff. Smiley visited: Turkey Shore Rum Distillery, in Ipswich, Massachusetts; Ryan & Wood Distillery, in Gloucester, Massachusetts; and Thomas Tew Distillery, in Newport, Rhode Island. Each distillery has their own intriguingly new methods and equipment to produce some of the very best rum that has ever been distilled. And learn how rum is moving onto a whole new level of excellence in this exciting revolution of new rum distilleries.

THE BASICS OF RUM PRODUCTION

Rum, by definition, is the aromatic spirit obtained exclusively by the fermentation of cane sugar in its various forms (e.g. molasses, sugar, cane juices), and distilled at less than 96% abv so as to retain the natural organoleptic properties of the raw materials of the sugar cane.

There are four basic processes involved in making rum: fermentation; distillation; aging; and, vatting. Fermentation is the process of yeast metabolizing available sugars and producing alcohol. The basic ingredients for fermenting a rum mash are: a source of cane sugar, water, nutrients, and yeast. The most commonly used sources of cane sugars are either the juices squeezed from sugar cane plants or molasses. The yeast selected for fermentation is important both for its production of alcohol as well as its roles in the development of the rum's flavor.

Distillation separates the alcohol and flavors from the fermented mixture to make the actual rum. Rum is distilled in pot stills, reflux columns or continuous columns operated in a low-separation mode, so as to retain the key impurities which define rum's flavor and character. Distilling equipment and methods vary from distillery to distillery thus producing rums with different characters.

Aging rum in barrels began as far back as the sixteen hundreds when rum was carried on long voyages in wooden barrels on merchant ships. People noticed that the rum from those barrels were greatly improved over its raw form and that it possessed a darker color that was very attractive. From this time on, distilleries began routinely aging their rum in barrels. Amber and dark rums are usually aged in used oak barrels to mellow and mature their flavor. Even white rums are often aged in oak barrels, but afterward, they are treated with a specially formulated activated carbon that removes all the color and lightens the flavor.

Although the lubricious effects of barrel aging are not fully understood, there are three broad categories of processes taking place in the barrel: the extraction of wood constituents imparting color and flavor; oxidation of the congeners in the spirit through the porous wood; and, reactions between the various congeners in the spirit and the constituents of the oak. Once maturation is complete, most rums are vatted or blended and some get an infusion of cane spirit caramel to adjust the final color of the spirit. Ultimately the process of vatting different rums together is how most distillers distinguish their own specific brand of rum. For a complete description of the difference between blending and vatting see Chapter 9, "Maturation, Blending & Vatting."

What follows is a detailed description about how to produce rum, from selecting a sugar source to bottling the final product. Some of the valuable information included outlines "traditional" rum production techniques. It is important to remember that traditional is just that..."traditional." There are always ways to improve. Many of these traditional techniques and procedures developed when little was known about organic chemistry and fermentation management. Additionally, many older distilleries were forced to use whatever equipment was available or could be cobbled together.

Because fermentation and distillation are both an art and a science, it is suggested that the reader seek out current sources of information about fermentation science and sanitary practices. The reader can learn a lot from the approaches developed by the wine and beer industries regarding these topics.

Ultimately the authors hope that this book can help you think through the technical and esoteric choices of ingredients, yeast strains, methods of distillation, and maturation that will allow you to make a high quality spirit that is well balanced, distinctive and fits your production capacity.

—*Ian Smiley*

PART ONE

Historic and Contemporary Rum Producers

Some claim that rum is the purest spirit of all since it is fermented directly from a pure sugar source rather than a starch, which has been converted to sugar prior to fermentation.

— *Chapter One* —

THE STORY OF RUM

Michael Delevante

Rum has been the drink of the famous and infamous. It was served to Captain Morgan and his band of pirates and used to complement the lime cure used by the British sailors to ward off scurvy. More has been written, good and bad, about rum than any other alcoholic distillate; and it is now ranked as one of the most acceptable, popular and certainly the most versatile spirits. While it is associated with the West Indies, one must realize that sugar cane, the source of rum, was a major crop in the Philippines and North Africa before Columbus brought it to the New World. Similarly, a variation of rum was probably made in India and Southwest Asia since the Middle Ages. Columbus, during his second voyage in 1493, took sugar cane from the Canary Islands to Hispaniola, which the colonists developed into a flourishing crop.

The first sugar factories were built in the New World early in the 16th century and sugar was first exported to Spain from Hispaniola in 1516. Spanish colonists crushed the juicy stalks of this member of the giant grass family to produce a sweet liquid with about 14% sugar and then let it evaporate in the heat of the sun or boiled it to produce syrup with a higher concentration of sugar. The liquid was then allowed to cool and crystals of sugar were formed in a mother liquor known as muscovado. However, turning the juice into crystals was not an efficient operation; the quantity of sugar crystals recovered was small in comparison to the mother liquor or sweet molasses that came as an unwanted by-product. The resulting molasses was fed to the slaves and cattle or returned to the fields as fertilizer. Disease and the brutal conditions of slavery in the cane fields quickly decimated the native inhabitants of the islands as European demand for sugar increased.[1] The nascent sugar industry grew to meet the demand by importing thousands upon thousands of African slaves

---

1 At the time of Columbus' arrival, the West Indies was home to a number of distinct cultural groups such as the Arawaks and the Caribs, from whom the Caribbean gets its name.

to plant and harvest the crop. Eventually, large sugar cane plantations were established by the Spanish, French, Dutch and English on Barbados, Haiti, Puerto Rico, Jamaica, Cuba, and most of the other Caribbean Islands.

Because early methods of sugar extraction were inefficient, any molasses not disposed of right away would begin to ferment by the action of the natural yeast in the air. This self-fermented residue of the sugar cane process became quite popular and its use as cattle feed or fertilizer soon diminished. It was not much longer until this fermented molasses was distilled into a stronger liquor. This early form of rum was also made from fermented cane juice but by all accounts these crude distillates smelled and tasted quite foul.

In 16th century Europe, it was not the custom to drink spirits for pleasure and most distillates were produced from wine by alchemists who used the product, aqua vitae or water of life, for medicinal purposes. The French referred to these medicinal products as eaux-de-vie. The Scots and Irish called it uisge beatha or usque baugh in Gaelic, which was later anglicized into "whisky." In the 17th century, distillation of various fermented crops became popular and spirit production was no longer the exclusive right of the alchemist. The century saw the growth in the production of brandy, whisky, gin, and later, rum.

The English colonists developed the production of sugar cane spirit made from cane juice with molasses added in the fermentation. It had several names, such as eau-de-vie de molasses (French), aguardiente (Spanish) and, more descriptively, kill-devil since it was the drink of inferior people, that when drunk in large quantities inevitably led to the demise of the consumer. The earliest derivative of the present name was rumbullion, which was described as a hot, hellish and terrible liquor. Many other titles existed for sugar cane spirits but, by the 19th century, "rum" became the internationally accepted name. However, in French it is spelled "rhum" and in Spanish it is spelled "ron."

Rum did not enjoy popularity amongst the "cultured" spirit drinkers since it was probably too sweet in comparison to whisky and gin but it was used extensively as a flavor for pastry and ice cream and in the tobacco curing process. Rums also became popular in cocktails such as punches, shrubs, and flips. The hot rum toddy was thought to be a cure-all for catarrh, colds and even for headaches if used externally to cool the forehead. It was also flavored to hide the rough taste; dark rum to this day is heavily colored with cane spirit caramel and may contain fruit essences or other flavorings.

The rum industry has grown as a result of several factors, many being quirks of fate. The World Wars greatly reduced the production of alcoholic beverages in Europe so West Indian rums came into their own as the main supply of uplifting spirits during this period. Prohibition in the United States and the growth of tourism, especially in Cuba, exposed the population to the new lighter rums that were being produced there. The old image of rum as a dark, sweet tonic-like product has long been dispelled; today, aged rums have gained the same social status as Scotch and other traditional spirits.

Some claim that rum is the purest spirit of all since it is fermented directly from a pure sugar source rather than a starch, which has been converted to sugar prior to fermentation. Rum has also come a long way in cleaning up its reputation as a sweet drink that is loaded with esters and other congeners. Aged white rums are usually purer than whisky and bear little resemblance to rumbullion, a thick, dark, and nourishing beverage (due to the addition of molasses), with a foul taste. The aroma of rum does not linger with the consumer as it did up to recent times and its social acceptability is mainly due to the sophisticated methods of fermentation and distillation employed by present day distillers.

The making of rum is one of the simplest processes in the alcohol beverage industry but there are several variations in the methods of fermenting molasses and distilling the ferments. Each rum producer has its own unique system of production which has resulted in literally hundreds of different variations in the flavor and bouquet of the finished products. This sets rum apart from say whisky, which tends to be similar within its country of origin; rums from one small producing country may be as dissimilar as whiskies produced in Canada and Scotland. It is of interest to note that highly refined rum, known as molasses or cane spirit, is as neutral and tasteless as the purest alcohol made from grains, and some of the best vodkas and gins are made from this spirit.

Certain rums or rum types have been linked to various countries; it is generally agreed that Jamaica is famous for the full (high ester) and medium-bodied rums while other producers are recognized for light rums. Bacardi, the largest producer in the world, has made a great success of its white rum and most distillers have switched to this style of rum, which is only slightly more flavorful than vodka. Jamaica still manufactures the high ester rums but these products are used for flavoring lighter spirits produced in other countries and as confectionery rum. In Japan, rum is used mainly in pastries and for flavoring.

Some rums are flavored with additives such as sherry and prune wine and colored with cane spirit caramel or burnt sugar. The prune wine additive dates back to the old days when rums were aged in the presence of prunes or similar fruit which created a style of fruit-cured rums. Today distilleries are independent from the sugar factories and many sell their products to independent blenders who blend and market rums for local and international markets. Caribbean rums, unlike most brands in Jamaica, do allow for the addition of up to 2% flavoring materials if the rums are exported to countries that allow flavors to be added. The rum must be distilled at less than 96% alcohol but again this is difficult to detect or enforce especially when the United States requires a maximum distillation strength of 95% alcohol. U.S. regulations also state that a flavor added to rum must have the flavor named on the label.

Barbados rum is produced from molasses and is distilled in either pot or continuous stills. The pot still product is a more flavorful and richer tasting rum than its continuous still counterpart; both are generally of medium body. Many of the better pot still rums of Barbados are generally consumed on their own. They were sometimes referred to as sugarcane brandy but this was obviously a marketing gimmick that has been discontinued since the word "brandy" should not be used in connection with anything but a fruit distillate. The rums of Barbados are world famous and Mount Gay, a name that dates back to 1663, is said to be the oldest rum brand in existence. Most of their rums are vatted from double-distilled pot still rums and lighter continuous still rums. Barbados makes a near neutral spirit on a column system that formerly produced grain spirits for commercial use and Canadian whisky.

Demerara rum is produced by the distillation of molasses in either pot or continuous stills. Fast fermentation with high amounts of yeast at fairly high temperature (32°C), tends to inhibit the development of many of the flavoring materials. As a result, the rum is much lighter in taste than the dark color would indicate. The coloring is achieved after the distillation by the addition of cane spirit caramel. The pot-still Demerara rums contain more esters and aldehydes and hence have much richer flavor and aromas than the continuous still products. Demerara is more a designation of where the rum is made (as is Demerara sugar) than it is a style of rum.

A type of rum, referred to as high wine, is also made in Guyana which, like most locally consumed rums, may have fruit extracts (prune etc.)

added during or after aging. Guyana, up to recently, operated an original wooden Coffey still but equipment has been updated in recent years and a modern bulk handling facility built in 1978 has helped to increase their exports to Europe, Canada, and other parts of the world. Dark Guyana rum, colored with cane spirit caramel, is still popular as a base for the dark Navy rums.

Haiti produces very high quality rums in much the same manner as France produces its cognacs and brandies. High quality sugar cane juice is slowly fermented by special yeast cultures and double distilled in pot stills. Some of the producers even pasteurize the juice before fermentation in order to destroy any bacteria that may compete with the yeast. The rums of Haiti are usually medium-bodied with a highly flavored, well balanced taste.

Dominica, Antigua, and Grenada islands in the West Indies have small privately owned distilleries that operate in unique ways. In Grenada and Dominica the owners control sugar cane plantations; all the cane is used to provide cane juice, which is fermented in wooden vats and distilled in a batch rectifying still. The rum is sold on the local market basically as an unaged product. In Antigua, molasses is imported and distilled in column stills to produce relatively light, aged and unaged products. Belize and Surinam are similar to Guatemala, Nicaragua, and Panama which are now producing light products which have become quite prominent in world markets. Ecuador produces mostly unaged spirit popularly known as Aguardiente. There are the usual exceptions since some distilleries in these countries also use local or imported molasses as a substrate as opposed to straight cane juice.

Martinique and Guadeloupe, which supply large quantities of rum to France, produce approximately 55% of their rums from molasses, while the remaining 45% is made from cane juice. The molasses-made rums are slow-fermented with the addition of dunder and distilled in pot or column stills. The cane juice rums are also slow fermented (sometimes with the addition of dunder) and distilled in both systems. Exports to France, grew during the 19th century when French brandy production was reduced to a trickle as a result of vine diseases oidium and phylloxera. Rum exports increased again during World War I when France had to devote its beet sugar to the production of industrial alcohol. Rums produced in these countries are classified by EEC regulations, which specify minimum congeneric contents for the distillates and they are referred to as "Rhum Agricole."

Mexico produces rums of light body, usually water white or light amber in color. These are made by the continuous still distillation of fast fermented molasses and are very similar to the Cuban and Puerto Rican rums. Large scale rum production is relatively new to Mexico since tequila was and still is the national drink. The growth of rum has been mainly due to the investment in large rum distilleries by Seagram's (now Diageo) and Bacardi. However, Mexico's strict environmental regulations have curtailed rum production in recent years.

Puerto Rico is the world's largest producer of rum and all are of light character. Puerto Rican rums owe much of their popularity to the improvement in quality as a result of research by Raphael Arroyo and the only rum pilot plant in the world, which is affiliated with the University of Puerto Rico. Their rums are produced from imported blackstrap molasses using cultured yeasts and distilled in multi-column stills. The rums are very light in body and taste and are water-white in color. The gold rums are usually a little fuller in body and taste and have a light amber color due to the addition of a small amount of cane spirit caramel. The first modern continuous still came into operation there in 1893 and exports to the United States started in 1897. Bacardi, which imports all of its molasses, is the largest producer of rum in Puerto Rico, and the world. Bacardi built its first distillery there in 1956 to take advantage of Puerto Rico's status as a US territory which exempted rum produced there from US excise tax.

Lighter flavored rums made popular by Bacardi are produced on a number of other islands in the Caribbean. St. Croix, also a US territory, produces large quantities of rum even while the distillery producing Cruzan rum has had many different owners in recent years. It is common practice in St. Croix, like in some other islands to dump its dunder out at sea. However, there is a limit on the volume that can be dumped which effectively caps their production capacity. Cuba, in partnership with Pernod-Ricard as its distributor, is expanding their rum facilities even though the main brand, Havana Club, is restricted from importation into the US.

The rums of Trinidad are made from imported molasses. These rums are generally light in color and of medium body and flavor. Their rum business was secondary to sugar in the early days of production and the early rums were mostly made with pot stills. Trinidad, famous for its Angostura bitters, modernized rum production in the 20th century and discarded all the old pot still methods. Like other West Indian producers, it no longer depends on local molasses, since the island's last sugar fac-tory was recently closed. Angostura, which owns other West Indian and foreign distilleries, currently operates the only distillery on the island. It has the advantage of using locally produced oil and the effluent from the distillery is treated in the local sewage facility in Port of Spain, the capital city.

Canada and other countries can produce rums that are distilled from imported molasses. Unlike Scotch and other spirits with a geographical heritage, rum can be made in any country even if they do not have sugar cane production. The cost is relatively competitive with imported rums since energy costs are lower which compensates for the extra freight pay-able on the molasses. Bear in mind that the freight cost on molasses is 50% more than the finished product since it takes 1.5 liters of molasses to make a liter of rum.

Most Canadian bottled rums are a blend of molasses based neutral Canadian spirits and imported West Indian rums. The latter, which plays the same role as rye flavor in Canadian whisky, provides the flavor while the neutral cane spirit provides the backbone of the blend. It is possible to produce flavored rum in Canada by altering the method of distillation but this is not common. The Canadian content is made neutral by dis-tilling on a 3 or 4 column distillation system and it is sometimes indis-tinguishable from grain neutral spirits.

There is an agreement between West Indian and Canadian rum pro-ducers that governs the marketing of "Canadian rum." This relates to the type of scene depicted on labels. It should not be tropical and the proto-col statement on labels must indicate the quantity range of imported rum in the product. An example is the statement "blended and bottled under Canadian government supervision," which implies an imported content of anywhere between 9.09% and 25%. It is unlawful for a Canadian distiller to bottle a pure imported product (liquor boards may) and the lowest domestic content for bottling in bond is now 1.5%. Rums with this domestic content can declare the product as imported. Rums from Puerto Rico and St. Croix however can be bottled as 100% imported as a result of the North American Free Trade Agreement between Mexico, Canada, and the US. It is fair to say that Canadian rums are as authentic as the imported rums, since the method of manufacture is identical to that used in the traditional rum producing countries.

Other countries famous for their rums are India (probably the largest consumer of rum), Mauritius, Nepal, and Brazil. Brazil uses cane juice or molasses to produce fuel ethanol and cachaça. Cachaça, although not classified as rum by Brazilians it does deserve mention. The cane that makes this product is not burned before harvesting; fresh cane juice is used within 24 hours of the crush. Natural yeast is used for a fast fermentation (to make a clean product) which may only last for about 24 hours. Some brands are distilled in small pots stills (to 76% alcohol) with the normal heads and tails cuts. Column still products are distilled to 96% alcohol from molasses wash, fermented by pure culture yeast; these distillates can also be blended and most are sold unaged but some brands are aged for one to five years. It takes approximately 1000 liters of cane juice to produce 100 liters of cachaça at 50% alcohol. Current estimates are that over 1 billion liters of cachaça are made in Brazil each year.

Rum is now produced or blended in many countries throughout the world that have never grown a stick of sugar cane. Even though this chapter does not include them all, it is sufficient to say that most producers now employ the same methods described above. And the rum industry will continue to grow as long as the world production of sugar cane is maintained at a level sufficient to produce the molasses required to supply the needs of the industry.

— *Chapter Two* —

ON SITE WITH
NEW ENGLAND DISTILLERIES

Ian Smiley

From the 1600s into the 1800s, New England was famous for, among other things, making some of the best rum in the World. But, by the end of the Prohibition the rum distilleries were mostly gone, rum production became focused in the Caribbean, and New England rum distilling had become all but forgotten for many decades.

However, in recent years rum production in New England has been experiencing a renaissance. Rum distilleries are popping up all over New England, and in many other places in the United States, and there is a strong affinity to returning to the heritage and tradition of New England's rum-distilling glory days. Almost all the new rum distilleries have developed their methods and rums based on some aspect of the history and lore of early colonial rum distilling. But, they are not stuck in the past! Each one of the new rum distilleries has employed some new technology or modern equipment that enables them to achieve a traditional rum with the benefits of modern spirit production. And, the results they are achieving are superb, and are occurring at an amazing rate.

In the following pages we will explore three of these new distilleries and see firsthand how they are rapidly returning the region to its previous status of producing the finest rums in the world. Ian Smiley went on site at these three distilleries and personally interviewed the people and here is what he learned.

TURKEY SHORE RUM DISTILLERY
www.turkeyshoredistilleries.com

Turkey Shore Distilleries is housed in a 5,000 Square foot facility in Ipswich, Massachusetts, and is owned and operated by Matt Perry, Evan Parker, and their dog Tank. In 2013 they had five different bottlings.

Turkey Shore pot still

Turkey Shore bottles— five variations of their Old Ipswich Rum.

Turkey Shore Rums

Old Ipswich White Cap Rum— a white rum that won a Bronze Medal for the Rum Category at the American Distilling Institute's 2012, 6th Annual Judging of Artisan Spirits. This wonderful white rum is made from Grade A molasses and is distilled and filtered multiple times to achieve a balance of purity and flavor. The Grade A molasses and Turkey Shore's proprietary yeast strain combine to form a smooth rum with floral and vanilla notes. They derived the name from the tempestuous seas that define New England's coastal living.

Old Ipswich Tavern Style Rum— an amber rum that won a Gold Medal, Best of Class for Amber rum, and Best of Category for Rum at ADI's 2012 Judging. It also won a Gold Medal for amber rum at the 2012 Ministry of Rum competition. This rum is a more refined rum as a result of aging in new American white oak barrels. It combines the flavors of the White Cap Rum with the robust contributions of oak aging.

Old Ipswich Greenhead Spiced Rum— a seasonal spiced rum available from May through September. Using the White Cap Rum as the base, Greenhead Spiced Rum is steeped with fresh lemon grass, green tea, and fresh spearmint. It is named after the infamous pesky flies that infest the East Coast from mid-June until the end of August.

Old Ipswich Golden Marsh Spiced Rum—a seasonal spiced rum available from October on through the winter months. This unique rum won a Silver medal at the Ministry of Rum competition in 2012. Golden Marsh is a blend of the white rum and some aged rum along with 10 other spices and zests.

Copper retort and high-efficiency shell-and-tube-condenser designed to look like an old-time thump keg and flake stand.

Lab & Cask Reserve Rum— was designed as a sipping rum, aged in 5-gallon barrels and bottled from single barrels at 86° poof (43% abv).

How Their Rum is Made!

Like most new American rum distilleries, Turkey Shore has adhered to traditional methods of rum production, while integrating modern technology to ensure efficiency and control over their processes.

Ingredients

Old Ipswich rums start out with activated-carbon treated water, and top-quality Grade A molasses, the same as you would pour on your pancakes or use to make muffins or molasses candy. The molasses is diluted with the carbon-treated water to a concentration optimum for the fermentation process. Since straight molasses and water are lacking in nutrients, they add yeast nutrients to aid fermentation along with their proprietary yeast strain.

Their fermentors are 500-gallon open stainless-steel totes that are beautifully designed and stackable. They ferment at 92°F (33.3°C) and use thermostatically-controlled immersion heaters to carefully maintain this temperature. A warm fermentation like this encourages the formation of esters and flavor components that give their rums the richness and complexity for which they are known. The molasses mash is fermented for a leisurely 9 to 12 days, which enables the development of a mature and balanced flavor profile. The final mash is about 8% alcohol.

The Still

Turkey Shore's rum still was custom made by Vendome Copper & Brass Works, who have been making stills for over 100 years in Louisville, Kentucky. The Turkey Shore still is a modified Scottish malt whisky style still, and has a capacity of 330 gallons.

The exterior of the still is modeled after a historic still documented in Ipswich on Turkey Shore back in 1770, but under the covers it is a state of the art steam-heated artisan pot still. Hidden inside the column are four bubble-cap trays, and inside the barrel on the left, which is made to look like an old thump keg, is a 50-gallon copper retort to increase the vapor separation and the purity of the product. Inside the barrel on the right, which is made to look like an old-time flake stand, is a modern high-efficiency shell-and-tube condenser. The retort and the shell-and-tube condenser hidden in the barrels can be seen from above in the adjacent picture.

Distillation Process

Turkey Shore's rums undergo two distillations: a wash-stripping run and a spirit run. For the wash-stripping run, a 330-gallon batch of fermented molasses wash is loaded into the still, the retort is bypassed so the vapor goes directly from the kettle to the condenser, and it is distilled until the low wines (i.e. the output from a wash-stripping) are down to about 32% alcohol by volume. There are no cuts taken during the wash-stripping, the entire output is collected and put aside for the spirit run. Each batch yields about 80 gallons of 32% abv low wines. They run four batches like this to accumulate about 320 gallons of 32% abv low wines to go into the spirit run.

For the spirit run, Matt and Evan clean out the still and empty the 50-gallon retort. They place about 320 gallons of 32% abv low wines in the still kettle (which totals 102 gallons of 100% alcohol), and fill the retort with about 20 gallons of 50-60% abv first-tails from the previous spirit run. First-tails will be explained in the following paragraphs. The total alcohol in the kettle and retort is about 112 gallons.

When the spirit run comes to temperature, the first 5 gallons or so of distillate are the heads. At the end of the heads phase the percent alcohol of the incoming spirit comes down to about 82% abv, at which point they cut to the hearts phase. The hearts are run until the percent alcohol of the incoming spirit drops down around 60% abv, at which point they cut to the tails phase. This cut is decided based on how the incoming spirit tastes towards the end of the hearts phase. The hearts are the rum, and they end up with about 110 gallons of around 75% abv rum. The first 20 gallons of tails are set aside to be used to fill the retort for the next spirit run and has an alcohol content of about 50% abv. After the first 20 gallons are collected the incoming spirit is usually around 30% abv and the rest of the tails phase is run into a separate receiver until it is no longer practical to expend the energy to extract more alcohol. At the end of the tails phase the incoming spirit is usually about 5% abv, and the still is switched off. The receiver typically contains about 10 – 20 gallons of about 15% abv late tails at the end of the run. At the end of the spirit run, the retort still contains 20 gallons but it is only about 4% alcohol. The contents of the retort are then discarded.

As can be seen above, there are two tails phases: the first tails phase is run until they have enough to prime the retort for the next spirit run; and, the second tails phase is just to recover the last of the alcohol and the flavor in the still kettle. The second tails are mixed with the heads and rectified in future distillation runs. However, at the time of writing, Turkey Shore did not have an economic use for the late tails and were terminating their spirit runs immediately after collecting the first 20 gallons of tails required to prime the retort for the next spirit run.

The following shows the composition of the output of a spirit run and a summary of the process:

Begin-cut	Head temp 172°F, incoming spirit at 82% abv.
Hearts End-cut	Head temp 190°F, incoming spirit at 60% abv.
1st Tails End-cut	Head temp 200°F, incoming spirit at 30% abv.
End-run	Head temp 208°F, incoming spirit at 5% abv.
Heads	5 gallons, 84% abv.
Hearts	110 gallons, 75% abv.
1st Tails	20 gallons, 50% abv, run until enough to prime the retort.
2nd Tails	10-20 gallons, 15% abv, mixed with heads and rectified in future distillation runs.

Barrel Aging

Before the advent of micro-distilleries in America, rum was almost exclusively aged in once-used charred white oak barrels for about six months to a year. Some rums are aged longer but in general, rum is not aged as long as whiskey or brandy. Used whiskey barrels have been an obvious choice for this, however many of the new rum distilleries popping up today are using new charred oak barrels to age their rum. And, like some of these new distilleries, Turkey Shore uses new barrels to age their rum.

They use 5- and 15-gallon new medium charred barrels from the Barrel Mill in Avon, Minnesota. Their barrel-aged rum is proofed down to 60% abv and aged for six to twelve months. All of Turkey Shore's Lab & Cask Reserve Rum and Tavern Style Rum are aged in new charred oak barrels but on rare occasions they reuse select barrels for conditioning.

That said, their oak aging works remarkably well. The new oak contributes a distinct oak character that initially strikes the drinker as not being true to style for a rum, but is excellent. Most of the new rum distilleries are using some new oak, and a pronounced oak character is rapidly becoming a familiar characteristic for US craft rum.

At the time of writing, there were not any real high-end US rums on the market. It can be expected that the new rum distilleries like Turkey Shore will lead the development of high-end rums that are on a par with single malt scotches and single barrel bourbons. In fact, Lab & Cask Reserve, Turkey Shore's recent release of a fine sipping rum, is an early entry into the market for this new standard of rum. Currently, Lab & Cask Reserve is only available in-house by the 5-gallon single cask.

Vatting

Turkey Shore does not blend their rum with any other rums or cane neutral spirits though they do vat together different barrels of their own rums. Most large-brand rum distilleries add caramel to their rums to mellow the flavor and to adjust the color. This is never necessary with Turkey Shore rums since the new oak aging contributes ample color and flavor mellowing components. However, in the future, they are considering production of a black rum which requires the addition of cane spirit caramel.

Next door to Turkey Shore Rum Distillery is a brewery, namely Ipswich Ale Brewery. They are working with this brewery to produce a custom ginger beer to blend with their future black rum product to make a dark and stormy cocktail. The dark and stormy was a drink coined by the British Navy in the late 1800s just after they purchased a ginger beer plant in Hamilton, Bermuda. They started mixing rum with the ginger beer and the cocktail came to be called a "dark and stormy" because of its association with the sea, and the name has never gone away. To this day you can get a dark and stormy cocktail in most bars in the Eastern United States, and of course in Bermuda. Individuals and cocktail bars will be able to blend these eminently compatible libations to make an excellent dark and stormy cocktail.

Filtering, Proofing, and Bottling

The fresh new-distillate is proofed down with Reverse Osmosis (RO) water to its 60% abv barrel-aging strength. If the rum is to be turned into finished white rum it is then passed through a coarse (4 – 8mm) bed of activated coconut carbon before it is either bottled as White Cap Rum or blended with barrel-aged rum to make their Tavern Style Rum. Before being bottled, all their rum passes through a series of one-micron cylindrical cartridge filters to ensure a crystal clear product free of any suspended particles. Most of the Turkey Shore rums are then proofed to 40% abv (80° proof) and bottled in antique bulge-neck 750mL bottles.

RYAN & WOOD DISTILLERIES

www.ryanandwood.com

Ryan and Wood Distilleries is housed in a 4,800 Square foot facility in Gloucester, Massachusetts, and is owned and operated by Bob Ryan and David Wood.

Ryan &Wood Folly Cove Rum

Folly Cove Rum, an amber rum produced from the finest quality table molasses, fermented, and then distilled in their classic German artisan pot still. Folly Cove Rum is aged in charred white oak barrels to achieve its distinctive flavor. Once properly aged, the rum is bottled by hand at their distillery in Cape Ann.

Folly Cove, along the Gloucester coast is rich in history and famous for its many shipwrecks. Smugglers of all types came to this cove seeking safety, only to find they were dangerously off course. Now, it is known for scuba divers searching for shipwrecks and lobstermen plying their trade. Folly Cove is one of the most beautiful areas of Cape Ann's coastline.

How Their Rum is Made!

To make their spirits, they use top-quality molasses along with modern yeasts and nutrients to ensure efficient and consistent results while adhering to traditional recipes. After the fermentation is done, they distill their spirits with their Holstein artisan pot still. With the Holstein, they have the flexibility of running it in a high-separation mode to render grain neutral spirit for their vodka and gin products, or they can run it in one of the various pot-still modes and preserve all the delicate flavors and aromatics of their rum and rye.

Ingredients

The water used to make the Folly Cove Rum is a combination of city water and the still's egress chilling water that are settled and then treated with activated-carbon. The water is then blended with top-quality

Left to right— Doug Ryan, Bob Ryan and David Wood.

Affectionately known as The Spirit of Cape Ann *(or Annie for short).*

table molasses to a Brix of 18 – 20 (~ SG 1.075). Lallemand Fermaid K yeast-nutrient and Lallemand EDV-493 Rum/Molasses yeast are added to ensure a solid and efficient fermentation with an optimum flavor profile for rum. They do not use any dunder in their rum mash, but they do use some in their yeast starter.

They have two fermentors: 550- and 600-gallon dairy sediment tanks. They ferment 450-gallon batches in them, which gives them three distillation runs per batch. They ferment at 90°F (32.2°C) and they do not require any heating or chilling to maintain this temperature. The warm fermentation encourages the formation of esters and flavor components that give their rum richness and complexity. The rum mash ferments in 4 or 5 days and produces a 9 or 10% abv wash.

The Still

The Ryan & Wood still is an artisan pot still made by Arnold Holstein GmbH in Markdorf, Germany. Their Holstein is a 150-gallon, two-column, 16-tray, steam-heated system, with a bell expansion chamber, a dephlegmator and a catalyzer at the top of the second column. The 16 trays are across the two columns: twelve in the first column; and, four in the second column. This gives them the flexibility to run with both columns engaged, just one column engaged, or neither column engaged. Also, there is a lever at each of the four trays on the second column that enables them to bypass individual trays allowing them to fine-tune the separation level to achieve exactly the desired proportion of aromatics in their spirits. Additionally, this flexible design enables them to produce each of their spirits in a single run.

When they make their rum they bypass the first column and run with just the two lower trays engaged in the second column. This affords enough separation to hold back the unwanted congeners while allowing a rich blend of aromatics through to the distillate.

Distillation Process

As mentioned above, Ryan & Wood distill their Folly Cove Rum in a single distillation run. They set the still up for a run by loading it with 150 gallons of fermented molasses wash, bypass the first column and run with just the second column. They run cooling water to the shell-and-tube condenser and the dephlegmator, and then they set the steam pressure to 0.2 Bar.

Initially, they engage all four plates on the second column and turn on the water flow to the dephlegmator relatively high so it condenses most of the vapor rising from the boiler. The purpose for this is to run with a comparatively high-level of separation until the heads are run off. This concentrates the unwanted early congeners into the heads phase thereby minimizing the amount of product lost to the heads.

Once the heads have run off, they switch to the hearts phase and disable the top two plates. They slow the water to the dephlegmator so as to reduce the reflux and allow the rich aromatics through to the distillate. After the incoming spirit is down to 72 – 73% abv they cut to the tails phase.

The heads and tails are mixed together and cycled through future rum distillations. They recycle this heads and tails mix, known as feints, about ten times and then they discard them and start over. The tails are run until the incoming spirit is down to about 9 or 10% abv, then the system is switched off.

The following shows the composition of the output from a rum distillation as a summary of the process:

Begin-cut	incoming spirit at 84% abv.
End-cut	incoming spirit at 72 – 73% abv.
End-run	incoming spirit at 9 or 10% abv.
Heads	2.7 gallons, 90 – 92% abv.
Hearts	10.5 gallons, 77% abv.
Tails	12 – 14 gallons, 40% abv, mixed with heads and used in future rum distillations.

Barrel Aging

Ryan & Wood proofs down their new-make rum to 120° proof (60% abv) with spring water before going into a combination of new and used barrels. They mature some of their rum in 15, 30, and 53-gallon new charred American white oak barrels, from the Barrel Mill, for six months. They also mature some of their rum in once-used 53-gallon Jack Daniels barrels, which they buy from Bluegrass (now Brown-Foreman), for 18 to 20 months. And a third portion of their rum is matured in their twice-used barrels. This system allows them to use and reuse barrels multiple times in their aging regimen to vary how much the wood interacts with and influences their rum.

When their barrels are used up and no longer suitable for aging spirits they take them to their brew-on-premise site where they use them to age bock and porter beers. After the brew-on-premise is finished with them they chop them up to make barbeque wood which they sell. The bags of chips sell very well and there are two restaurants that buy them for their open-pit beef cookers.

Vatting

Ryan & Wood does not blend its rums with anything, but they do vat them to achieve the best taste and consistency they can. They vat their rum by mixing 20% of their new-oak aged rum with 80% of their used-oak aged rum. Nothing is added, such as caramel color, because their color has always been good. However, in the future they are considering production of black rum which will require the addition of cane spirit caramel.

Filtering, Proofing, and Bottling

After the rum is barrel-aged they add activated carbon to it just prior to plate-filtering and bottling. The rum is filtered in a two-stage process: it is first passed through a 2-Micron plate filter just prior to vatting; and, then it is proofed down to 40% abv with distilled water and then passed through a 1-Micron plate just prior to bottling. For bottling, they use a manual gravity bottling line with six filler heads.

NEWPORT DISTILLING COMPANY
www.thomastewrums.com

The History of Rum in Rhode Island

As the sugar trade grew in the American colonies in the early 18th century, so did the production of rum. In those days, rum distilling was done mostly in the New England colonies and in particular, Newport, Rhode Island. By 1769, twenty-two distilleries were operating in Newport and it had established itself as the rum capital of the world. Using blackstrap molasses, pot stills, and local water these distillers created a flavorful rum that was enjoyed throughout the world.

However, the second half of the 18th century proved to be much more difficult for the industry. First, the Sugar Act of 1764 increased the cost of getting sugar and molasses from the Caribbean. Second, as one of the cities that was occupied by the British during the revolution, many of the merchants that made and traded rum in Newport fled their homes and businesses. Finally, by the turn of the century, settlers had moved west and began to turn their corn and barley into whiskey which was a much less expensive spirit.

By 1817 only two distilleries remained in Newport. Economics, changing tastes, and political turmoil had taken its toll and in 1842, John Whitehorne went bankrupt and the final rum distillery in Newport closed. Shortly thereafter, in 1872, Rhode Island's last distillery, the John Dyer Distillery in Providence, shut down.

For 135 years the once thriving Rhode Island distilling industry lay dormant. Finally, in 2007, Newport Distilling Company received the first license to distill in the State since the close of the John Dyer Distillery. Naturally, the goal was to recreate the rum that had been world famous 250 years ago. Using the same blackstrap molasses, local water, and pot still techniques, this rum has been resurrected and is now called Thomas Tew Single Barrel Rum.

History of Newport Distilling Company and Thomas Tew Rum

Newport's reputation for fine rum is well deserved. Although the last of the 22 rum distilleries in Newport closed down in 1842, the history and tradition surrounding Newport rum has remained. Part of this history includes Thomas Tew, who, during the rise of rum in Newport, was immortalized as "The Rhode Island Pirate." A sailor all his life, Tew had a lifelong career of privateering and pirating that took him from the Colonies to Europe, Africa, and back. Although no one knows where he was born, it is known that he called Newport, Rhode Island his home, and trading and drinking rum was an essential part of his life at sea. Now, after three centuries, Newport is home again to this icon and his famous spirit.

Newport Distilling Company grew from a brewery that was started in 1999 by four graduates from Colby College in Waterville, Maine, namely Brent, Derek, Mark, and Will. Their brewery is called Coastal Extreme Brewing, or The Newport Storm Brewery as it is known by many.

In April of 1999, they moved into a 2,500 square-foot facility in the Middletown Tradesman Center, and on July 2nd 1999 the brewery's first beer, Hurricane Amber Ale, was released. In 2002, the brewery expanded into an additional 1,000 square feet, and in 2006 they started Newport Distilling Company to make Thomas Tew Single Barrel Rum, thereby bringing back this historic practice to Rhode Island. They were able to make use of much of the same equipment they had for their brewing, such as fermentors, pumps, and tanks.

The brewery and distillery were such a success that in 2010 they built a brand new, 8,000 square foot facility in the North end of Newport which allowed them to add a beautiful visitors center and tour deck. This also afforded them the opportunity to upgrade their equipment from the used equipment they started out with in 1999.

Newport Distilling Company Rum

Thomas Tew Single Barrel Rum, is inspired by the craftsmanship of the past. It is slowly made in a small pot still to replicate the rum which would have been produced in Newport in the past. The still, along with the dark molasses, temperate climate, and local water combine to create a spirit that has not been available for over a century. One sip of this flavorful, dark rum and you will wonder how this tradition could have ever disappeared.

HOW THEIR RUM IS MADE!

To make their rum, they only use blackstrap molasses and local water, the same as the old-time rum distilleries of two and three centuries ago. And, with their brewery on the same floor as their distillery, they have an ample supply of brewers' yeast slurry available to ferment the molasses. After the fermentation is done, they double distil the molasses wash. The stripping run is done in their 300-gallon Artisan Still Design wash-stripper and the spirit run is done in their Christian Carl artisan pot still. The new-make rum is then proofed down and aged in used bourbon barrels.

Ingredients

Thomas Tew Rum is made using only simple, natural ingredients: water, blackstrap molasses; and, ale yeast slurry. The mash water is made

Newport Distilling's 105 gallon pot still designed by Christian Carl.

by filtering local city water through an activated-carbon filter and a fiber filter. Following that, the water's mineral content is built up with gypsum. Then, enough blackstrap molasses is mixed with mash water to yield an Originating Gravity of 1.125. To ferment this mash, they use the left-over yeast slurry from the fermentation of their Hurricane Amber Ale. No yeast nutrient is added but a large dose of yeast slurry is used to ensure a solid, fast fermentation. No dunder is used in their rum mash.

Their fermenter is a 2,000-gallon stainless-steel conical unitank fermenter in their adjacent brewery with a chilling jacket and temperature control. They ferment at 80°F (26.7°C) and it takes three days. The Terminating Gravity is between 1.060 and 1.053. The reason for such high Originating and Terminating Gravities is because the blackstrap molasses they use has a larger concentration of cane solids (non-fermentable dissolved solids) compared to a Grade A molasses. Despite the Specific Gravity starting out at 1.125 and ending at around 1.057, the alcohol content of the wash ends up being about 9% abv. Between the blackstrap molasses and a fairly high fermentation temperature, a lot of flavor components and aromatics are produced resulting in the rich, complex flavor, characteristic of Thomas Tew Rum.

The Stills

The Newport Distilling Company has two stills: a 300-gallon Artisan Still Design wash stripper designed in Lethbridge, Alberta, Canada and fabricated in China; and, an artisan pot still for their spirit still made by Christian Carl in Germany. Their Carl is a 105-gallon, single-column, 4-tray, steam-heated system, with a dephlegmator. Each of the four trays can be engaged or bypassed as required.

This four-plate design gives them ample control over separation level so they can produce their rum with the desired level of aromatics for the flavor profile of their rum. Also, the temperature-controlled flow valve on the chilling-water supply to the dephlegmator enables them to maintain a specific temperature in the dephlegmator, thereby affording very consistent results from one run to the next. Using modern artisan stills allows them to consistently and efficiently recreate a centuries old rum style.

Distillation Process

Thomas Tew Rum is double distilled. The first distillation is the wash-stripping, which is done in their 300-gallon stripping still. For each wash-stripping run, a measure of hearts from a re-distilling of the feints

Thomas Tew Rum is aged in once-used 53-gallon bourbon barrels from Woodford Reserve.

collected during the the spirit runs is added to the wash. All the alcohol and the aromatic congeners in the fermented molasses wash are concentrated into a smaller volume at a higher percent-alcohol in the low wine that results from this wash stripping. The stripping still is sized to produce enough low wine to fill the spirit still for the second distillation called the "spirit run". The low wine is about 50 to 55% abv.

Unlike more neutral spirits, the second distillation is to polish the spirit while retaining flavor. Further distillation would simply take out the flavors that were so carefully crafted from the molasses during fermentation.

For the spirit run, the low wine from the wash-stripping is loaded into the still kettle, the still is set up with all four trays engaged, the water to the shell-and-tube condenser and the dephlegmator is turned on, and the water flow to the dephlegmator is set to hold the dephlegmator water at about 68°F. The steam pressure is set to 0.2 Bar.

As with all spirit runs, the first distillate is collected as heads. Once the heads have run off, they switch to the hearts phase. The percent alcohol of the incoming spirit stays in the low 90s and high 80s for the entire heads and hearts phases. The head temperature at the begin-cut to hearts is about 173°F (78.3˚C) and it begins to rise from that as the tails phase begins. At the time of the begin-cut, the temperature controller for the dephlegmator water is set to about 105°F. By running the dephlegmator water at such a cool temperature during the hearts phase, there is sufficient reflux going on at the plates that the percent alcohol of the incoming spirit remains very high throughout the run. Newport Distilling can afford such an intense hearts phase because the wash, which was fermented from blackstrap at a high temperature, is full of rich flavor components. The end-cut to the tails is determined by the rise in head temperature at the end of the hearts phase. And the tails are run until the incoming spirit is down to about 10 to 20% abv, then the system is switched off.

The following shows the composition of the output from a spirit run distillation as a summary of the process:

Begin-cut	incoming spirit at 90% abv.
End-cut	incoming spirit at 90% abv.
End-run	incoming spirit at 10 to 20% abv.
Heads	2 gallons, 91 – 92% abv.
Hearts	30 gallons, 90% abv.

Tails   10 – 15 gallons, 50% abv, redistilled and used in future primary
                 distillations.

The tails are collected and when a sufficient volume is accumulated
they are redistilled, and a portion of the hearts from this re-distillation are
incorporated in each future wash-stripping run. The heads and tails from
this re-distillation are discarded.

Barrel Aging

Thomas Tew Rum is aged in once-used 53-gallon bourbon barrels
from Woodford Reserve. The new-make rum is proofed down to about
110° proof (55% abv) before going into the barrels. This comparatively low barrel proof results in a higher contribution of wood character
since less proofing down is required at bottling time. The cask strength of
about 110° proof (55% abv) and the bottling strength of 84° proof (42%
abv) were specifically selected to optimize the extract from the barrels and
balance the flavor on the palate.

Thomas Tew is a single barrel rum. Unlike many aged spirits, flavor
is used to determine whether a barrel is ready rather than a calendar.
Small changes in the wood and the distillate create differences in aging
times. By continually tasting each barrel, Thomas Tew is bottled when it
is ready, no sooner no later. This takes at least two years with most taking
three or four years, and often more. Some Thomas Tew is in the barrel
for five years.

Vatting

Thomas Tew is single barrel rum and is not blended with anything.
Thomas Tew Rum is made from start to finish in their Newport Distillery. No outside source of aged rum, raw rum, cane neutral spirit, or caramel is used in Thomas Tew. Only rum made from the fermented molasses
at their facility is used to produce this spirit.

Filtering, Proofing, and Bottling

After the rum is barrel-aged it is proofed down to 84° proof (42% abv)
and filtered through a 1-Micron fiber cartridge filter. The rum is then
bottled using a manual six-head gravity filler. Each bottle is hand-dipped
in sealing wax, and numbered. Thomas Tew Rum is a truly hand-made
spirit!

PART TWO

How to Make Rum

Rum, like other distilled spirits, is made from a small number of raw ingredients yet the variety of choices among sources of sugar, types of yeast, and whether one decides to use cane spirit caramel to adjust the color, all play a role in determining the character of the rum.

— *Chapter Three* —
EQUIPMENT

Ian Smiley

FERMENTORS

Rum is traditionally fermented in simple open fermentors, which may incorporate chilling coils to keep the temperature from getting too hot and killing the yeast (i.e hotter than 105°F, 40°C). Also, rum distilleries would want to keep the fermentation temperature within a consistent range so as to produce a consistent product. Most rum fermentations are held between 80 and 90°F (27-32°C) and chillers are required to do this. However, if the batch size is 50 gallons or less, then chilling may not be required.

A lot of the artisan rum distilleries that have sprung up recently are using open totes as their fermentors. These are affordable, work remarkably well, come in a broad range of sizes, and are optimized to conserve space. They are stackable and can be easily moved around with a forklift. They can also be fitted with tri-clamp connectors and valves to enable hoses and pumps to be attached so the mash can be easily transferred to the still or other containers.

STILLS

Rum is distilled in many different types of stills, all of which are functionally pot stills of some sort or another. Larger rum distilleries use continuous-run column stills, but even these are operated so as to draw the spirit off numerous trays down the column in order to collect what is effectively a pot-still spirit.

The pot stills that are best suited to making rum are ones that achieve a slightly higher level of separation than the stills used to make brandy or whiskey. For this reason, rum is generally distilled to a somewhat higher proof than fruit or grain spirits. Where grain and fruit spirits distil out to between 65 and 70% abv, rum typically distills out to between 70 and 80% abv.

In a traditional pot still used for making rum, the middle component is a thump keg with a separator chamber above it. This thump keg is called a "retort" in rum-making parlance. The retort and separator chamber literally effect a second distillation on the vapor which results in a higher proof distillate. Other rum pot stills have two retorts, again resulting in a higher proof distillate than most other pot-still designs.

Given the higher level of separation that rum stills generally have, it is very common for rum to be made with a single distillation. This preserves more of the flavor and aroma over double distillations.

A typical grain or fruit-spirits still would usually go straight from the lyne arm to the condenser, and not have the retort and separator in between. Some rum distilleries do use these non-retort types of stills and they generally do double distillations in deference to the lower separation level.

Barrels

Most rum is aged in oak barrels to smooth out the flavor and add character, and almost all rum distilleries employ once-used barrels for aging. Though, rum aged in new charred barrels is rapidly growing in popularity. The most common once-used barrels for aging rum are used bourbon barrels. However, others such as any used American straight-whiskey barrels, sherry barrels, and wine barrels are also used. If rum were aged in new barrels the rum would take on too much oak character to remain true to style for what people have come to expect of a rum flavor. However, there are several rum distillers that use new charred-oak barrels to age their rum, and this rum is really quite excellent in its own right. The flavor has been very well received. It has a distinct bourbon-like flavor to it since it is, in effect, aged like bourbon in a new charred-oak barrel. This flavor works very well with rum, and even though it is not typical, it is very nice and makes good rum for sipping or in mixed drinks.

Rum is normally aged for a few months to a couple of years in barrels. Unlike the many years that whiskey or brandy takes to age in oak, rum does not require this much oak contact. Rum can stand on its own without any aging at all, but nowadays most rums are aged for at least a few months on oak to smooth out the rough edges that are characteristic of freshly distilled rum.

An important consideration when barrel-aging spirits is the size of the barrel. Distilled spirits are usually aged in 53-gallon barrels, and a barrel of that size has a certain area-of-oak to volume ratio. The larger the barrel the lower the area-of-oak to volume ratio, and vice versa. A lot of artisan distillers prefer to age their rum in smaller 15- and 20-gallon barrels because these are more compatible with their batch sizes. But, this means a significant increase in area-of-oak to volume ratio over that of a standard 53-gallon barrel. This is like increasing the quantity of an ingredient in a recipe. The smaller barrels will impart considerably more oak constituents and the rum will taste different. This is not to say it will not be good but it will be different.

Now, many experts in the whiskey industry have claimed that the standard 53-gallon barrel is technically too big and therefore has a somewhat too low an area-of-oak to volume ratio. This has resulted in most distilleries having to add oak staves to the contents of their barrels to impart more wood character. The oak in some barrels is rich enough that they don't require this, but many do. This has led to experimentation with smaller barrels like 40 gallons and 30 gallons, and so on. Different distilleries have arrived at different conclusions, but a good number of Scottish malt whisky distilleries have concluded that 20 Imperial gallons (roughly, 25 US gallons) is the ideal size for aging malt whisky.

The reason for using the aging of Scottish malt whisky as the example here instead of bourbon is because Scottish malt whisky is aged in once-used barrels the way rum is, whereas bourbon is aged in new barrels. So, the observations made by Scottish malt whisky distillers are more directly relevant to aging rum.

We know 53-gallon barrels work for aging rum since most distilleries have been using that size for centuries, and we have it on good account that 25-gallon barrels work remarkably well for aging spirits in once-used barrels, so a safe conclusion could be drawn that barrels for aging rum should be once-used bourbon barrels and have a capacity of no less than 25 gallons and no more than 53 gallons. Of course, this is not a hard and fast rule, but it would make a good starting point for a new artisan rum distillery.

— *Chapter Four* —
RAW INGREDIENTS

The following is a brief description of some of the raw ingredients available for rum production and their effect on the final product. Rum, like other distilled spirits, is made from a small number of raw ingredients yet the variety of choices among sources of sugar, types of yeast, and whether one decides to use cane spirit caramel to adjust the color, all play a role in determining the character of the rum.

SUGAR CANE

Cultivation of Sugar Cane and the Production of Molasses
The cultivation of sugar cane is quite standard around the world so a general description will apply to the methods used by all sugar producing countries.

Sugar cane is said to have originated in New Guinea and was introduced at least 8,000 years ago as a garden plant for chewing. It then migrated around the world by the dispersal of stem cuttings with manual cultivation and weeding. The transition to a field crop probably occurred in India several centuries before the Christian era. The first positive evidence of sugar in a solid form dates back to A.D. 500 in Persia. By 1600, the production of raw sugar in tropical America was said to be the largest industry in the world and the relationship between slavery and cane cultivation is well known.

Sugar cane is a giant grass belonging to the genus saccarum; there are many varieties that result from the several types of seedlings, climates, methods of cultivation, and hybridization that have taken place over the ages. Cane, up to 1887, was always grown from cuttings but it was discovered that the flower contains a valuable seed from which seedling cane can be grown.

Commercial cane is propagated by means of cuttings or whole stalks planted in furrows with a light covering of soil. Each plant produces shoots, or suckers, which form a clump or cane stools. The ripening of cane is dependent on soil conditions and rainfall and this may vary from 10 months to 2 years, depending on the geographical location of the crop.

In the West Indies, the harvesting season takes place after a 12 month period of growth. After cutting, usually by hand, new plants called ratoons spring up from the stubble to produce a second crop that may, in turn, produce up to 7 years of cane from the same planting. Traditionally the cane was burnt prior to cutting in order to remove the leaves and kill hornets but it must be harvested within 24 hours in order to reduce deterioration in the sugar content and the formation of dextrins, long chain sugar molecules that are not recoverable as crystals. The heavy skin on the cane does provide some protection to the pith. In areas with low labor cost, hand cutting is still practiced but elsewhere it has largely been replaced with mechanical harvesting.

The harvested cane is then hauled to the central sugar factories, by various modes of transport, for grinding and conversion to sugar and molasses, the byproduct used in most rum production. The grinding season in the West Indies begins in January and ends in May or June, depending on the capacity of the factory or acreage of the fields. The cane contains about 75% water, 10 – 16% sugars and 10 – 16% fiber. The latter, known as "bagasse" with a moisture content of about 50%, is used as a fuel in the sugar factory boilers. The sugar content should be less than 2% if proper grinding conditions are met.

The sugar making process is very complicated but it basically involves the mechanical chopping of the cane and squeezing out the sweet juice using up to 6 sets of roller mills. Lime (calcium hydroxide) is added to the juice which is heated and clarified to remove all the undesirable solids (field mud, etc.) so that only clear juice enters the evaporating system. The evaporators produce syrup with about 30% sugar and this is mixed with sugar crystals (known as low grade sugar), which provide a nucleus for the dissolved sugar to grow on. This mass of fine crystals and the sweet syrup is then boiled under vacuum (i.e. at a low temperature to avoid caramelization) until the crystals grow to the desired size. The contents of this boiling pan, known as "massecuite," are then emptied into a large vessel, called a crystallizer, and cooled for a period of 6 – 8 hours. Here the crystals increase in size and the mass is then emptied into a high speed centrifuge that separates the crystals from the mother liquor. The centrifuge is similar to a washing machine where the basket retains the crystals and the molasses passes through the holes to be stored for another boiling.

The sugar obtained in the first centrifuge is called A sugar and the liquid, A molasses (or high test). The latter still contains dissolved sugar (about 70%) and fine grains so it is boiled again to recover more crystals (called B sugar) in a second centrifuge and molasses with reduced sugar content is separated again. The second stage molasses also has a relatively high sugar content so it is boiled again, cooled and centrifuged to recover low grade sugar (fine crystals) and blackstrap molasses with a sugar content of about 55 – 60%.

The fine crystals are mixed with the original syrup to restart the cycle and the molasses is used for making rum, ethanol for fuel or cattle feed. The raw sugar can be used as is or refined to make white granulated sugar, which again yields molasses since raw sugar is merely a white crystal coated with a fine layer of molasses. The ash content of the final molasses may, with the advent of mechanical cutting and harvesting, be as high as 12%; this is not good for fermentation since it increases the osmotic pressure on the walls of the yeast cell which impedes the activity of the yeast. Some distillers may add raw sugar to the molasses to lower the ash content; the incremental cost may be offset by the increased yield, especially when the shortage of molasses drives up its price. Cane juice is not used as much as molasses for making rum since it is more economical to process the juice and sell the granulated sugar and the molasses. The major exception to this is that cane juice is commonly used for rum in the French islands and in Brazil for cachaça. However, there are some distilleries that do use a small percentage of juice in the fermentation since the bacteria and wild yeast in the freshly squeezed juice do tend to produce more flavorful rum. Molasses is now a valuable commodity and the price, due to its demand for making fuel ethanol, has more than doubled in the last 5 years.

The variety of cane, if molasses is used as a substrate, has no influence on the quality of the rum; the influence of juice if boiled prior to fermentation may also be negligible but fresh squeezed cane juice with its indigenous wild yeast can influence the taste of the distillate if pot still distillation is used to make the rum. The water used for diluting the molasses may have more impact than the molasses. This effect would also be negligible if the dilution water is purified, say through a reverse osmosis unit.

A hectare (2.471 acres) of prime land normally yields up to 125 tonnes (2204 lbs./tonne) of cane which, in turn, produces about 12 tonnes of sugar and 1,600 liters of molasses containing up to 60% of dissolved sugar. Thus, 1,600 liters of blackstrap will produce up to 600 liters of absolute alcohol. These are theoretical numbers; yields may vary with soil, climatic, and cultivation methods.

Beet sugar, which accounts for about 40% of the world sugar production, can be used for making ethanol but not for the production of rum. The standard of identity for rum states that it must be made from the fermentation of cane juice or the by-product of cane sugar manufacture. Sugar producing countries would have wanted it to also state that rum must be produced in cane growing countries but the standard makes no such claim. Consequently, rum can be produced in any country by merely fermenting imported molasses. Beet molasses is not as rich in sugar as cane molasses.

Flavor Effects of Various Sugar Cane Byproducts

The intensity of the rum flavor is dependent on the proportion of cane solids in the mix, therefore the more cane solids in the mix, the more intense the rum flavor. Since cane solids are concentrated in the molasses component of refined cane products, straight molasses and water would yield a very rich rum flavor. Whereas a mash of ¼ molasses and ¾ white sugar would produce a much milder-flavored rum.

In broad terms, cane juice could be said to be comprised mostly of water, then sugar, and lastly cane solids. Molasses on the other hand is a blend of sugar, cane solids, and some water. This is why there are different grades of molasses. A grade molasses, which has a higher sugar-content and a lower cane-solids content, is sweeter and more pleasant to eat than lower grade molasses that have a lower sugar content and a higher cane-solids content. Higher grade, i.e. sweeter molasses is often called "Grade A" whereas lower grade molasses is called "black strap". Most black strap molasses is bitter and not generally considered preferable for human consumption, and is usually relegated to livestock feed. This is because black strap molasses has more cane solids and less sugar.

Since lower grades of molasses have higher concentrations of cane-solids they contribute a very intense rum character, which makes them well suited to increasing rum flavor. That said, a distiller must bear in mind that lower grades of molasses have much less sugar in them and may require significant sugar additions in order to produce a sufficient yield.

Individual distillers can adjust the proportions of molasses and sugar to their preference. Also, raw cane sugars such as demerara, turbinado, or simply brown sugar are types of sugar that still have molasses left in them in varying proportions, and are sometimes used to make rum. However, many new rum distillers find that blending molasses and white sugar affords easier control over the proportion of cane solids.

Since different cane products are comprised of different concentrations of sugar, the amount of water used to dilute them varies considerably from product to product. As a general rule, the cane products must be diluted with enough water to bring the Specific Gravity (SG) down to about 1.060, or 15° Brix. However when using cane ingredients that involve significantly less molasses (<45%) and appropriate nutrients, a specific gravity of up to 1.080 may be set which will give an increased yield and a more refined flavor.

Characteristics of Molasses

	GOOD	POOR
Brix	87.60	88.20
Total sugars as invert %	57.97	49.93
True sucrose %	36.44	34.61
Reducing sugars %	19.61	13.50
Ash %	7.31	11.57
Total Nitrogen %	1.10	0.45
Total Phosphoric Acid, as P2O5 %	0.19	0.21
Gums %	2.00	3.75
pH	5.50	6.30
Total sugars : ash ratio	7.93	4.31
Reducing sugars:sucrose ratio	0.54	0.39
P2O5 : total nitrogen ratio	0.17	0.47
Gums : total sugars ratio	0.03	0.08
Titratable volatile acidity	<5000 ppm	>5000 ppm
Bacterial content	<500 cfu/gm	>1000 cfu/gm
Natural aroma – steam distillation	good	indifferent

Source: Arroyo, R. "Manufacture de Ron – 1938"

A total sugars-to-ash ratio of 6.5:1 is preferred because too much ash negatively affects yeast activity. Whereas a total sugars-to-ash ratio of 4.5:1 is only fair, and anything below 4.5:1 is poor.

WATER

Clean, microbial free water is essential since adding bacteria to the ferment will counter the effectiveness of the molasses pretreatment. However water containing bacteria may produce a distillate with desirable characteristics; this however is difficult to control and distillates may vary from batch to batch. It is safer to use clean water. Too high a mineral content in the water (especially salts of calcium and magnesium) will raise the ratio of non-sugars to sugars in the wash and be a detriment to the growth and activity of the yeast. Inhibitory effects of various salts may create long fermentation times and high residual sugars. Non-sugars will also foul the still.

The water chemistry for a rum mash is not as critical as that of other mashes since there are no enzyme conversions or extraction processes that could depend on the presence or absence of certain ions, or the pH of the substrate. However, there is an optimum mineral composition and pH that will result in better fermentation and flavor profile. The optimum water chemistry is roughly the same as that for an ideal whiskey mash. A hardness level of 4; almost no iron; 100 ppm calcium; 50 ppm magnesium; about 200 ppm sulfate; and a pH around 6.5.

Water is also the primary source of oxygen required by the yeast during the initial, aerobic reproduction phase during fermentation. The water for a healthy fermentation should have a generous amount of dissolved oxygen in it. Since a rum mash is not cooked or boiled prior to fermentation, the way whiskey or beer mash is, there is generally little need to take any steps to ensure there is an ample supply of dissolved oxygen in the mash water. Water from municipal water supplies or natural sources of water tend to have an ample supply of dissolved oxygen. However, the distiller should be aware that if the source water is for some reason lacking in dissolved oxygen it will be necessary to aerate the water.

Water can be aerated by sloshing it around vigorously. For example, it can be transferred hard from its source to the fermentor. Also, a compressor can be used to bubble sterile filtered air through an aeration stone for about 30 minutes. If the water is being delivered to the fermentor from a tap with a faucet aerator screen on it, this will supply all the dissolved oxygen required. If the water is being delivered by a hose, the hose can be oriented so that the water falls and splashes hard into the fermentor.

YEAST

Selecting a Yeast Strain

The ideal rum yeast must generally: produce a fair yield of alcohol in a reasonable time; produce a distillate with rum characteristics; be a good producer of congeners and fusel oils; in the case of high ester rums, withstand a considerable concentration of fatty acids; and withstand a higher degree of ash in the substrate.

The yeast for making rum should be a strain that produces a lot of flavor and have a strong ester profile, such as a whiskey, schnapps, beer or wine yeast. Also a yeast strain should be selected based on the type of wash to be set. Sterilized wash, partially sterilized wash, or unsterilized wash are the various choices but the latter is more common.

Saccharomyces cerevisiae, which is the same yeast used in wine and beer production, produces the most predictable and manageable fermentation. Within this yeast family are many different strains that produce different outcomes, some of which should be avoided because they do not metabolize simple sugars very well. Generally, most wine strains that are alcohol tolerant can work well for rum given the right addition of fermentation nutrients.

Brewing yeasts like top-fermenting ale yeasts are good for making rum and they are well worth experimenting with. However, since ale yeasts are acclimated as maltose fermentors, they will require substantial nutrients to perform well, particularly the ones that are known for producing strong ester profiles. Also keep in mind that most beer strains begin to slow in fermentation performance after 5.5-6% abv.

A number of distillers have had wonderful results using whisky yeast strains as long as they are fermented in the proper temperature range to appropriate alcohol levels. These originally were beer yeast strains that have been acclimated to tolerate higher alcohol levels. There are also more specific yeasts that were created to ferment other sugar sources like beet sugar that do very well in a rum wash.

Example strains of yeast that can be used for making rum are the Fermentis whiskey yeasts, such as Red Star 43106 as well as Safwhisky M-1 yeasts, Lallemand EDV-493 Rum/Molasses yeast, EDV 46 cane molasses yeast and K1V 1116 high-ester wine yeast. The Red Star is a common bourbon and Canadian whiskey yeast, and the Safwhisky yeast is the original scotch whisky strain. Both are excellent for making rum and EDV-493 is becoming a widely used rum yeast with new micro-distilleries.

Another yeast type that is being used for making rum is mead yeast. A mead mash is actually a very similar substrate to a rum mash in that they are both basically a mix of a high-sugar syrup (i.e. honey for mead and molasses for rum) diluted with water to a desired specific gravity for fermentation. White Labs makes a sweet mead yeast called WLP720, which is well suited to making rum.

If using a liquid culture, it is best to propagate or purchase the appropriate amount of vital and viable yeast for the entire fermentation rather than to underpitch and essentially use your full fermentation volume as a propagation medium. If you use dried yeast strains at the appropriate pitching levels they will perform just fine without aeration. This is due to the way they are produced which is in a very high oxygen environment and they are produced with very thick cell walls to help them endure the drying process.

Highly congeneric rums have traditionally used a combination of wild yeast and bacteria to produce the necessary outcome dictated for that style. However, to achieve similar characteristics while introducing reliability and consistency as is experienced with using culture yeasts, commercially available blends that combine culture yeasts and bacteria may be used. It is to be noted that the introduction of bacterial cultures or yeast and bacterial blends into a distillery is not without peril. If your plant produces more than one rum type or other spirits that use culture yeasts alone, there exists the possibility that the bacteria may take over your plant. Impeccable sanitization and separate hoses and gaskets should be used to reduce the potential for cross contamination. If your plant uses open fermentation, it is best that the bacterial or/and wild yeast or commercial blend fermentations be conducted in a completely separated room.

Specific yeasts to avoid are those used to produce high levels of ethanol. A lot of packaged strains of yeast nowadays are specifically formulated to produce neutral ethanol with very low ester profiles. These are not suited to making rum since they produce ethanol with very little flavor. These strains are often sold, or referred to, as "turbo" yeasts. These strains were developed either for the fuel ethanol industry or for vodka production where high alcohol yield is the goal, not desirable flavor. This works fine for the aforementioned products because the rectification level is so high that any undesirable flavor is eliminated as a neutral spirit is produced. However, most craft distillers desire to make a rum with the best flavor possible, so the proper choice of yeast is crucial if that is the desired outcome.

YEAST AND ESTERS

The higher alcohols and acids produced by yeast cells play an important role in the production of flavor and aroma, both by themselves and through their combination to form esters (an acid + an alcohol = an ester + water). Ester and other congeneric levels can be increased with longer fermentation times, resting of dead wash, which is not recommended, or the use of less nutrient in the substrate. Experiments have shown that esters can be formed without the intervention of bacteria since ester formation is also related to the actively working yeast cell. Nutrients should not be slugged into the fermentor, they should be added gradually and ideally some should be held back for addition when the fermentation is half completed. Esters may also be formed during distillation of the wash by continued reactions with the alcohols and acids in the vapor phase.

Other Yeast Considerations

Some yeast strains take twice as long to ferment as others, the fermenting plant capacity must be designed based on this. Tolerance to heat is also a factor to consider. Therefore the type of cooling system is important. External plate heat exchangers are sometimes used for cooling but contamination can be a problem especially if one heat exchanger is shared between fermentors. The safest method is coil or jacket cooling using chilled water as a coolant.

A strong yeast culture must be used to overcome the effect of wild yeast and bacteria. It is essential to culture the yeast in stages and to not subject the culture to too large a batch of fresh wash. The final pitch should be 5 – 10% of the fermentor. It is felt that good quality rum, with the necessary congeners, can tolerate some bacteria in the ferment. Some bacteria do contribute to the aroma and taste of good rum and these are normally present in the molasses or even in the dilution water.

Rum yeasts can be isolated from the surface of the sugar cane (similar to the "bloom" on a grape) but careful plating out must be done to isolate a pure colony. Different rums can be produced from different yeasts or different wash recipes which may have cane juice added in the ferment prior to fermentation.

While a higher alcohol yield in the fermentor will require less steam and a smaller column for stripping alcohol from the wash, yeast is intolerant to alcohol above 20% because higher concentrations become poisonous to the yeast. Ash in the molasses also creates a high osmotic pressure on the cell wall which inhibits the efficiency of the cell. In molasses fermentation, 10% alcohol concentration is usually the maximum attainable due to the inhibiting effects of ash.

Finally, yeast obtains nitrogen by splitting off ammonia from the amino acids (present during the fermentation) through the degradation of proteins by proteolytic enzymes. When this splitting occurs, an alcohol or an acid is formed with one less carbon atom. The resulting aldehyde, R.CHO, forms an alcohol or an acid by reduction or oxidation respectively. Thus RCHO + O yields R.COOH and R.CHO + 2H yields R.CH2OH. R is an organic group which differs for each amino acid.

Nutrients

Rum washes, whether made from cane juice, molasses, brown sugar, white cane sugar or some combination, are by nature lacking in nutrients and the bio-materials needed to nourish a healthy yeast fermentation. A high sugar, low nutrient mash environment is very stressful for yeast and can create problems during fermentation. The total sugars should not exceed the ability of the yeast to convert these sugars to alcohol. However, as we dilute the sugar content, we are also diluting the natural nutrients in the source of sugar. High test molasses is usually more deficient in nitrogenous and mineral constituents than low test molasses. If we are fermenting molasses with a low sugar content (at normal brix) we should avoid high initial sugar concentration since this also increases ash and non-sugar components. The increasing ratio of non-sugar to sugar concentrations, as fermentation progresses, inhibits the activity of the yeast. A pure sugar fermentation is not that simple since there are no nutrients (nitrogen) in sugar. Therefore, supplemental nitrogen and other elements must be added since a rum mash is deficient in the nitrogen supplying nutrients (macro-nutrients) needed in the production of yeast cells during yeast reproduction. Other nutrients (micro-nutrients), like vitamins and minerals, further enhance the health of the yeast and the quality of the fermentation.

There are many yeast nutrients available and all are intended to make up for the natural lack of nutrients in the mash. Not all are created equal however, so you need to delve into their specific compositions to determine what might work best with your yeast strain and fermentation base. A recent innovation has been nutrients that work throughout the fermentation in a time release fashion. They release certain nutrients at the appropriate time during fermentation which helps maintain yeast performance even in the presence of elevating alcohol levels.

The nutrient blends like Fermaid K can be an excellent mix for rum fermentation since they contain a blend of macro- and micro-nutrients. An excellent nutrient mix can be achieved by using the following regimen:

Mix 2.5 Lbs of Go Ferm® per 1,000 gallons of cane substrate with the yeast at yeast rehydration.

Add 2 Lbs of Diammonium Phosphate (DAP) per 1,000 gallons of cane substrate. This must be added directly to the full mash volume. It must not be added to the yeast rehydration as it is toxic to the yeast at such a high concentration.

Add 2 Lbs of Fermaid K® per 1,000 gallons of cane substrate after 1/3 depletion of sugar. For example, if the OG of the mash were 1.060, the Fermaid K® would be added when the SG was down to about 1.040.

If the substrate has the benefit of a good nutrient mix, the fermentation time can be reduced to 72 hours from 96-120 hours.

However, if such blends are not available then Diammonium Phosphate (DAP) can be used alone. DAP is generally very easy to find, however it is important that it be commercial-grade DAP and not agricultural-grade. The agricultural grade is farm fertilizer and is not purified to a level that is safe for any beverage or food application, so it must be avoided. While DAP will work well, the fermentation may take a day or so longer since the mash is lacking in the micro-nutrients necessary to fully nourish yeast.

CANE SPIRIT CARAMEL

Cane spirit caramel is another ingredient used in the production of rum, though, unlike the others mentioned above, it is added before the rum is bottled. Many amber and dark rums are infused with cane spirit caramel after they are aged to adjust the color of the final product and it is typically incorporated during the blending process. Most rum distilleries purchase cane spirit caramel that is ready to use for infusing though it can also be made if necessary or desired.

To experiment with making the cane spirit caramel, mix about 3½ ounces of white sugar with just enough warm water to dissolve it then bring it to boil. Simmer the mixture gently until it begins to turn yellow. Continue to simmer but watch the color change carefully. The color will become a deeper yellow, then brown, then dark brown. For rum the cane spirit caramel must be burnt much darker than for candy apples, or other confectionery applications of caramel. When it is a light brown color, take it off the heat and continue to watch the color change. When the cane spirit caramel is a very dark brown, almost black, cool it in cold water to halt the burning. When cooled, this cane spirit caramel will be a very dark, hard, glassy sugar. If there is any black ash or carbon on the cane spirit caramel this would be an indication that the burning went too far.

— Chapter Five —
MOLASSES PRETREATMENT

STERILIZATION

It is a good practice to effect a complete or partial sterilization of the sugar source in order to develop a fine aroma during fermentation and to purify the raw material by removing non-sugars (mud/ash) prior to fermentation. Partial sterilization involves the destruction of microbiological flora but thermophilic bacteria will survive. The temperature should not exceed 185°F (85°C) or the sugars will begin to caramelize. In grain substrates pressure cookers are used to kill heat resistant spores (248-266°F, 120-130°C) but this is prior to the formation of glucose. It is only necessary to kill the vegetative spores in molasses so no higher than 185°F (85°C) should be sufficient. Proper fermentation conditions and viable yeast will overpower the remaining heat resistant spores.

Partial sterilization of high pH molasses includes the addition of sulfuric acid to lower the pH and water is added to reduce the brix to between 45 and 55 degrees. Hydrochloric acid is more expensive but it may reduce scaling in the beer/wash still (also known as an analyzer) since sulfuric acid does tend to combine with the calcium in the molasses to form calcium sulfate, which will precipitate on the column trays.

Steam coils or open steam can be used to increase the temperature for clarification to between 158 and 185°F (70-85°C); this temperature should be maintained for at least 30 minutes. The mixture can be centrifuged, an expensive method, or settled in batch tanks using an overflow system. But either way care should be taken when draining "mud" (which contains gums and ash) from the system because sugar can be lost during the periodic draining of the clarifiers.

MASHING

The mixture is then cooled in a plate exchanger, or equivalent, down to 95-104°F (35-40°C). Water is added to reduce the brix and the nutrients are introduced. Molasses, deficient in phosphoric acid should have a phosphate added but this is only necessary in the yeast propagation stage. The optimum amount of phosphoric acid (P2O5) should be 0.2 – 0.5% of the weight of molasses being used. Though P2O5 is rarely used if the pH of the wash is lowered with other acids. A ratio of 1:5 between phosphoric acid and nitrogen tends to be good.

If total nitrogen in the molasses is 1% or more, additional nitrogen may not be required. If nitrogen is 1% by weight of molasses, it will be necessary to add 0.2 – 0.5% ammonium sulfate or diammonium phosphate (DAP) based on the weight of molasses being mixed. A commercial yeast nutrient may also be added. DAP is more expensive than the sulfate but it may create less scaling in the stills. Sulfate or urea are used as cane fertilizer, the sulfate may contain sand as filler so DAP can be more beneficial. Urea is not recommended since it is responsible for the formation of the chemical ethyl carbamate (a carcinogenic agent also known as urethane) during fermentation and it can be carried over to the distillate in some distillation systems. The limit for urethane is in parts per billion. Too much nitrogen in fermentation can create excess ammonia in the dead wash which can affect the distilled product. A blue product may result from excess NH3 reacting with a copper still.

The introduction of oxygen into the pre-fermentation wash will lead to a lag in fermentation as the presence of excess oxygen causes yeast to go into their reproductive phase. The point is to ferment, not to generate unnecessary yeast mass. Fermentation takes place as an anaerobic process, so any oxygen introduction via pumping, recirculation, or stirring can result in a stuck fermentation and should be avoided.

Pretreatment tends to eliminate stickiness and foul odors in the molasses; it also decreases surface tension and viscosity. It biologically enhances the molasses, reduces fouling in the beer still (thus requiring less steam and cleaning time) and makes it easier to recover yeast bottoms (using decanters or centrifuges) and potash salts. Potash salts are soluble so they remain in the clarified molasses. Occasional experiments should be done to ascertain the correct conditions (pH, temperature, and brix) for effective pretreatment and clarification. pH values for different yeast strains lie between 4.5 and 5.5; a lower pH is required with non-sterilized molasses, but a higher pH may be acceptable with a sterilized substrate.

An optimal pre-fermentation wash pH is in the range of 5.0-5.2. The goal is to result in a fermenting pH in the range of 3.0-4.0. This drop will be achieved by the yeast. To adjust pH it is best to use food grade phosphoric or lactic acid. Also, citric acid can be used to reduce the pH but it is not as effective and requires greater amounts.

It is also recommend to invest in a lab grade pH meter that is automatically temperature correcting and has a replaceable probe. This style of meter can be calibrated before each use, using buffer solutions that are standardized to specific pH ranges.

You should avoid using pH papers for a couple of reasons. Pre-fermentation rum washes tend to be dark in color which makes accurate reading of the strips difficult. They are also not suitable when attempting to adjust the pH because their range is not narrow enough nor is their accuracy sufficient.

Molasses intended for industrial alcohol fermentation is set at a pH value so that no further increase in acidity occurs during the fermentation. For the production of rum, an increase in acidity due to fatty acid formation during fermentation may be desirable since they combine with various alcohols (especially ethyl) to form valuable esters. Rums fermented at high pH levels are more mellow and delicate; this is a problem if there is no facility to partially or absolutely sterilize the molasses beforehand.

Wash for the production of rum is set at a total sugar concentration of 11.0–13.5 grams total sugar/100 mL wash while yeasts available for industrial alcohol production will tolerate 15–16 gm sugars/100 mL wash. A higher incremental addition of sugar, as in wine making, can also be employed to achieve higher alcohol contents. The metabolic products of yeast can be toxic to the cells so high congeneric levels can hamper the efficiency of the yeast, whereas industrial fermentation with low toxicity can be more efficient. Thus setting rum fermentation at a high brix will be inefficient and total sugars in dead wash will increase.

Composition of Molasses
Before & After Pretreatment

(Calculated on original density values)

	Before	After
Brix	90.90	84.40
Total Sugars (as invert)	50.17	52.68
Ash (carbonated)	14.20	8.52
Gums	6.19	3.40
* Total nitrogen	0.55	0.95
* P2O5 (total)	0.21	0.23

* pH	6.10	5.20
Total sugars/ash ratio	3.53	6.18
Gums/total sugars ratio	0.12	0.06
P2O5/nitrogen ratio	0.38	0.24

* conditioned to approach optimal values

A proper mash
should have the following characteristics:

Brix	18 – 21
Titratable acidity	(in mL of 1/10 normal alkali/10 mL wash) = 2 – 3.5
pH value	5 – 5.5
Total sugars (T.S.)	(gm/100 mL) = 11.5 – 13.5
Nitrogen	(milligrams/100 mL) = 7.5 – 100
Phosphoric acid as P2O5	(milligrams/100 mL): 15 - 20

To calculate quantity of 88 brix molasses used to produce 1000 liters wash at 16 brix:

liters molasses x S.G. molasses x brix = liters wash x S.G. wash x brix

liters molasses = $\frac{1000 \times 1.0653 \times 16}{1.4686 \times 88}$ = 132 liters molasses (~188 kg)

This formula is a close aproximation and the resulting wash should be measured with a claibrated hydrometer or refractometer.

— *Chapter Six* —

FERMENTATION

Fermentations may be continuous, batch, or incremental. Each has its advantages but batch may be the most efficient if the wash is fed slowly to the fermentor with a strong yeast inoculum. Continuous fermentation requires less fermentors but it is prone to contamination which can affect the entire inventory of wash. Incremental is used to produce a higher alcohol content, such as in wine making, but the disadvantages are calculating the quantity of molasses in the wash and admitting cold, unfermented wash to a warmer environment in the second stage of addition. A batch system with 10% inoculum pitched when the brix has fallen by half of its original set brix should give a good yield of alcohol and acceptable fermentation efficiencies.

Steps for a Clean Fermentation

1   A proper yeast propagation system or a full volume pitch of liquid yeast or dry yeast.
2   Sanitary conditions in the fermenting room.
3   Clarification of molasses is desirable but not essential. It does serve to reduce calcium that was used in the juice clarification process.
4   Proper cleaning and sanitization of all piping, heat exchangers, hoses, pumps, gaskets and vessels that will be in contact with substrates and washes. This is true of CO_2 pipelines to a CO_2 plant, if applicable.
5   The correct acidity in the fermentor.
6   Proper temperature control of the fermentor and never allowing the temperature to decrease during fermentation.
7   Early distillation of the wash after fermentation.

A Suggested Yeast Propagation System
for Small Distilleries

Assume a fermentor with a capacity of 3000 liters:

Day 1: *(setting a yeast donor in the morning)*

Set a small stainless container or glass carboy with 10 liters of wash at 16 brix. Molasses and water should be mixed in the container since sterilization may be a problem. Quantities of each may be variable, depending on the brix of the molasses but assuming 88 brix molasses they will be about:

2.5 liters molasses + 7.5 liters water

Add sulfuric acid (approx 10 mL) diluted in water to give a pH of 4.7

Diammonium phosphate (DAP) – 4 gm

Magnesium sulfate – 3 gm (not mandatory)

Fermaid K or similar nutrient – 4 gm

Yeast (Danstil, Superstart or equivalent) – 4 gm

Mix with clean air or shake vigorously and seal carboy with cotton bung or gas trap. In 8 hours or less, it should fall to 10 Bx if kept at about 86°F (30°C).

Day 1: *(setting the day yeast tank in the afternoon)*

The yeast donor stage may be eliminated in which case dry yeast would have to be added to the day tank. An addition of about 75 gm yeast is recommended for 200 liters of wash.

Prepare a 250 liter day tank with 200 liters of wash at 16 brix.

Add sulfuric acid (approx 500 mL) to give a pH of 4.85 (dilute acid before adding). Quantity may vary with pH of molasses, and citric acid or hydrochloric may be used.

100 gm DAP

25 gm Fermaid K or similar nutrient

Inoculate with the contents of the 10-liter yeast donor when it has reached 10-12 brix.

Ferment at 86°F (30°C) until it reaches 10°Bx and then inoculate into the fermentor. This could be ready by the next day but times will vary with temperature of the ferment

Day 2: *(Setting the fermentor in the morning)*

Assume a 3000 liter fermentation tank which will hold 2500 liters of wash plus the 210 liters of yeast inoculum from the tank above. The tank should have an aspect ratio of no more than 2:1, that is, the diameter should be about one-half the height.

Set the fermentor with 2500 liter of wash at 16 brix. If molasses is low in ash (less than 8%), an 18 brix setting can be used. The dilution formula below can be used to calculate the approximate molasses to water ratio for a desired SG. These formulas are close aproximations and the resulting wash should be measured with a claibrated hydrometer or refractometer.

(Desired SG − 1) / 0.036 = Number of pounds of molasses per gallon H_2O to achieve the desired SG

In metric this would be:

(Desired SG − 1) / 0.030 = Number of kilograms of molasses per 10 liters H_2O to achieve the desired SG

Reduce to a pH of 4.9 with the chosen acid. Quantities of each may vary but hydrochloric is recommended. 5 liters may be adequate. Always add acid to water

DAP or ammonium sulfate − 1 kg

Add the contents of the day tank which should be at about 10-12 brix

When the fermentor has reached 12 brix, add another 1 kg DAP and 0.5 kg Fermaid K

The wash should not foam but if it does, add a small quantity of anti-foam to the fermentor. Margarine or cooking oil will also work.

CONTROLLING FERMENTATION TEMPERATURE

If your goal is predictable results it is best to control the fermentation temperatures of washes. The best results are derived using cooler, longer fermentations. By controlling the fermentation temperature you can control the level of esters being produced and in many cases you will derive a more complete fermentation. By controlling the ester production your head cuts will be reduced and flavor enhanced.

The best temperature for the fermentation of rum washes using culture yeast is 80°F (~26.6°C). At this temperature the yeast does not become stressed and its performance is maintained throughout the fermentation. There are strains that list a higher maximum temperature than 80°F, but the pitching rate usually has to be increased to counter the death rate and the flavor outcome is still different than sticking with the 80°F recommendation.

High fermentation temperatures can be caused by a number of factors. For instance, it is very important that any dunder sent to the fermentor, from the wash kettle, be cooled to at least the fermentation temperature before the yeast is pitched. Another fact to keep in mind is that yeast bioactivity can substantially raise the temperature in a fermentor. Therefore it is best to send the mash to the fermentor at 5 degrees below the targeted fermentation temperature. The bioactivity will raise the temperature to the fermentation temperature and then the jackets can easily maintain it. Either way, once the temperature rises it is very hard to control, particularly if you have external fermentor cooling jackets. If the fermentation temperature is not controlled, the yeast will become stressed due to osmotic pressure and a portion will die off. At best this will lead to a wash that takes a very long time to ferment out, and at worst, may not completely ferment out at all or be unusable. The latter would be due to the temperature being so high that the majority of the yeast culture is killed or badly mutated which can lead to both poor fermentation performance and create a high risk of bacterial infection.

Fermentation carried out at high temperatures 95-104°F (35-40°C) cannot be set with a high sugar concentration. Sugars can be increased if fermentation is carried out at lower temperatures. Ample supplies of yeast nutrients will also permit a high total sugar concentration in the wash. Among the elements most essential to the life of the yeast are carbon, nitrogen, phosphorous, zinc, and potassium, followed by magnesium, iron, manganese, sulfur, and calcium; deficiencies in nitrogen and phosphorous can be common in molasses.

In most cases at the recommended concentration and temperatures, a complete ferment can be achieved in 2-6 days. The alcohol content should be about 6.5% after fermentation and this should be checked (an ebulliometer or distillation is recommended) since this will evaluate the efficiency of the ferment and subsequent distillation. Also, if the fermentation is clean, the pH should be in the 4.1 – 4.3 range.

Maintain Sanitary Conditions

A new yeast inoculum is recommended for each fermentor but there are ways to cross inoculate if sterile conditions are maintained. The washing out of tanks is extremely important and a variety of products exist for this purpose. In the event of infection, usually demonstrated by excessive foaming in the fermentor, a sour, vinegar-like odor or a pH less than 3.9, various anti-bacterial agents may be added. These include penicillin and a commercial disinfectant known as Lactrol. These should be used only in extreme cases and with caution. A log sheet of fermentation results should also be maintained.

FERMENTATION PRACTICES IN JAMAICA

The following is a description of the process for making rum washes based on existing methods in Jamaica.

The fermentation process for the high ester rums is designed to produce a high concentration of congeners in the distillate; this is achieved by the introduction of bacteria and wild yeast to the fermentation, which converts the sugar to esters, acids and fusel oils rather than the normally predominant ethyl alcohol. The molasses is first diluted and mixed with cane juice skimmings and the refuse of the sugar cane after its juice has been extracted. This rather unpleasant looking mixture is placed in pits (known as muck pits) and left for six months to cultivate various strains of bacteria and wild yeast. The pits are never emptied. Small quantities are then added to a diluted mixture of molasses, cane juice, and dunder; this sets up the fermentation without pure culture yeast that may last for up to two weeks. The resulting ferment contains ethyl alcohol with a high concentration of butyl, amyl and ethyl acetates (esters), which is then distilled in an Adams pot still to produce so-called high ester rums; containing up to 1,600g of esters/100 liters of rum. Some distillers may also introduce milk of lye during fermentation which supposedly develops rum oils or fatty acids which are essential for the formation of some esters but this is only desirable in the production of high ester rums. Finally, aldehydes from a column still may be added during fermentation to increase the ester profile of the wash.

Medium-bodied rums are made by a cleaner fermentation where cultured or commercial yeast is added to a diluted solution of molasses with dunder (in some distilleries) being introduced to acidify the wash. In distilleries where cane juice is available up to 50% cane juice can be added to enhance sugars and reduce total ash. Cane juice, fresh from the sugar mill, contains wild yeast that will compete with the cultured yeast to convert some of the sugar in the molasses and develop the ester profile of the distillate. It is no longer economical or practical to ferment pure juice, although a few distillers in the Caribbean do this. There is also the option of mixing molasses with sugar in islands no longer producing cane since this may be more economical with the new price and scarcity of molasses. The above rums are usually distilled in pots but it is possible to make a medium-bodied rum on a single column still. However, this is not the practice in Jamaica.

The ester content of the distillate can be reduced further by blending light-bodied distillates with full or medium-bodied distillates, so that a wide range of rum types can be offered to blenders who use these products. High ester rums are also used by confectioners, manufacturers of aromatic flavors and sold to German as well as Austrian producers of rum verschnitt, a rum flavored spirit.

Normal blackstrap molasses contains up to 60% sugar (sucrose and inverts glucose and fructose) by weight. This is too concentrated for yeast so the molasses must be diluted with water in order to reduce the sugar content. As with all fermentations, roughly half of the sugar is converted to alcohol by the action of yeast so the sugar content in the molasses is reduced to about 16% by weight in order to produce a fermented wash with about 7% alcohol by volume. Higher percentages may be uneconomical due to the high ash content in the molasses and its effect on yeast activity but the potential admixture of sugar and molasses may allow for a higher alcohol yield.

During the sugar making process, lime (calcium hydroxide) is often added to clarify the cane juice; this gets carried over into the molasses that goes to the distillery. The calcium is removed (in some distilleries) by mixing the molasses with an equal quantity of water. The mixture is acidified with sulfuric or hydrochloric acid and heated to about 85°C (185°F). This is then pumped to clarifier tanks where the calcium settles out as calcium sulfate; it is insoluble at higher temperatures because it works on a reverse solubility rule. The cleaner, diluted molasses is then cooled and mixed with a quantity of water that is calculated to reduce the sugar content in the wash to 16% by weight (16 brix). The calcium sulfate and mud are dumped from the bottom of the clarifier tanks. Some distillers do not clarify the molasses since it is a costly process (molasses and hence sugar, does get lost in the dumping) but they could bear the consequence of a still that scales up every two weeks. Scaling can be reduced by proper sizing of the holes in the column plates, or feeding the wash at a temperature that is equal to the temperatures of the feed plate. This is not always easy since it requires proper sizing of the heating equipment.

The cooled, diluted molasses is then pumped to the fermentors where a nutrient such as ammonium sulfate or diammonium phosphate (sources of nitrogen for the yeast) and cultured yeast are added. The acid added during the clarification process provides the ideal pH for the yeast; some distillers may also add dunder (effluent from the beer column), which produces the same effect. Distillers who do not clarify their molasses usually use a combination of dunder and acid to acidify the wash prior to fermentation. Citric acid may also be used as a safety measure but it is more costly and less effective.

The cerevisiae type of yeast is used in clean molasses fermentations but there may be different strains used depending on the desired end product. A microscopic quantity of a pure culture from a test tube slant or lyophilized vial is propagated by exposing the cells to successively larger quantities of a sterilized molasses solution. A test tube of yeast may be added to 100 mL of the molasses solution. After 24 hours, this is added to 2 liters and this, after 24 hours of incubation, may be added to 400 liters of diluted molasses. The yeast cells multiply at a tremendous rate and within 24 hours this 400 liters can be admitted to a 9,000 liter tank (known as a bubb tun) of diluted molasses. The yeast is in its most active state when half of the sugar is used up. This usually occurs after another 12 hours in the 9,000 liter tank; at this time, part of the mixture can be added to a 100,000 liter fermentor. Sterile air is sometimes introduced to the propagation vessels since this promotes yeast growth; it is not necessary in the fermentor since there are enough yeast cells to convert all the sugar in the fermentor into alcohol and fermentation is an anaerobic process. In the production of baker's yeast, which is usually produced in a molasses solution, air is used since the object is to grow yeast rather than produce alcohol.

During fermentation, the sucrose is inverted to equal portions of glucose and fructose by hydrolysis (assisted by the acid medium) and enzyme activity. The yeast enzymes then convert these invert sugars to the alcohols and congeners via the Krebs cycle, which is a complicated diagram showing all the compounds and precursors formed during any type of fermentation. Fermentation efficiencies can be in the 90 – 95% range depending on conditions. This can never be increased since some of the sugar is utilized for yeast growth and there is some alcohol lost in the carbon dioxide especially if it is not scrubbed and collected.

There are many commercial yeast strains offered to the distiller. Some claim to achieve different flavors in the product or higher alcohol contents from a given quantity of sugar. However, there is a limit to the alcohol produced in molasses fermentation since, unlike grain ferments, the ash content of the molasses, which is greater in mechanically harvested cane, has a detrimental effect on yeast activity. There is a system where molasses is fed gradually to the fermenting tank. This has to be carefully controlled since over feeding of molasses may produce more alcohol but the yield or liters of alcohol per tonne may actually suffer. Incremental fermentation with the fermentor being set in two stages can also be tried but again, the control over the quantity of molasses used is difficult. A reasonable yield is about 270 liters of alcohol per tonne (1000kg) of molasses with 55% total sugars.

Continuous fermentation has also been practiced but the risk is contamination of a large quantity of wash if there is a problem upstream and therefore is not a common practice. Re-use of yeast after washing the cells has also been used but it is safer to start with a new culture in a batch system, again to avoid the risk of contamination. Fermentors after use are usually rinsed out with water or a weak solution of chlorine. A quaternary ammonium compound may also be sprayed on the walls of the fermentor but this must be rinsed off before the next cycle.

Heat is given off at a tremendous rate during fermentation (a fermentor may rise in temperature by at least 10°C during fermentation) so the liquid has to be kept at 30°C (86°F) for the duration by cooling the liquid, usually with coils in the fermentor or jackets on the tank surface. A fermentor with 100,000 liters at 16% sugar will contain 17,600 kg of sugar. The yeast consumes this in about 36 hours to produce about 8,800 kg CO_2 plus a similar quantity of alcohol.

It is also interesting to note that a test tube of yeast after the four stages of culture (which take four days) and no more than 2 days of fermentation ends up as a mass of yeast weighing up to 30 kg. This may be separated for sale as cattle feed but the fermented wash containing the yeast is usually pumped as is, to the distillation units.

This is, with minor variations, the type of fermentation used by all modern distilleries in Jamaica, but some may ferment to a higher or lower concentration of alcohol and clarification of the molasses may not be performed by all distillers. It is also common to use bakers' dried yeast, without the propagation stages listed above but this may reduce the normal yield due to the fact that cultured yeast is usually more efficient than a special culture of dry or compressed yeast added directly to the fermentor. If the distillery does not propagate its own yeast, it is advisable to add the commercial yeast in a bubb tun (the size depending on the fermentor) so that there is some acclimatization before subjecting the yeast to the final stage. The shape of the fermentor is also important but not critical. A cylindrical tank with an aspect ratio (height to diameter) of 2 to 1 is recommended. Wooden fermentors (Douglas fir), often found in Bourbon or Scotch whisky distilleries, are also used but cleaning and sanitation does pose a problem.

FERMENTATION RESULTS WITH GOOD MOLASSES

Initial Brix: 18
Final Brix: 5

Initial pH: 4.9 – 5.1
Final pH: 4.3 + 4.5

Total sugars (gms/100 mL): 12.76
Residual sugars (gms/100 mL): 0.60

Fermentation Times: 36 – 40 hours
Attenuation: 12.5

Alcohol: 7.50%
Gms alcohol/100 mL wash: 5.92

Alcohol yield on T.S. (total sugars): 46.45%
Fermentation efficiency: 95.67%

One tonne (1000kg) of cane will produce ~ 160 kg total sugars based on 16% T.S. in cane. 1 tonne final molasses will contain ~ 570 lbs total sugars based on 57% T.S. in molasses. Now 1 tonne of cane will yield ~ 36 kg molasses, which should yield 9.7 – 10 liters of absolute ethyl alcohol (LAA).

CALCULATION OF FERMENTATION EFFICIENCY

This can be done in several ways but the simplest way to calculate your fermentation efficiency is with the following formula. Find the difference between the total sugar before fermentation and the total sugar after fermentation, divide that difference by the total sugar before fermentation, then multiply by 100.

Thus: $\frac{(T.S.B.F - T.S.A.F)}{T.S.B.F.} \times 100\% =$ Fermentation efficiency

If the distiller does not have the means to test for total sugars a general rule is: Divide the actual volume of alcohol produced by the theoretical volume of alcohol expected, then multiply by 100.

$$\frac{V_{actual} \text{ of alcohol}}{V_{theoretical} \text{ of alcohol}} \times 100\% = \text{Fermentation Efficiency}$$

Some means of testing the alcohol in the wash such as an ebulliometer is needed for this calculation. A crude rule of thumb is for every degree drop in brix you should achieve 0.5% alcohol. If brix is set at 16 and the fermentor dies at 4, you should get about 6% abv.

— *Chapter Seven* —

DISTILLATION

The following is a brief description of several types of distillation methods used by rum producers around the world.

POT DISTILLATION

Simple Pot Distillation Systems

The first is a simple pot still where the fermented wash is, as in the case of malt whisky or brandy, distilled twice to produce a product with up to 75% alcohol. This produces a medium-bodied rum that can be used for vatting or blending with lighter rum spirits.

A second type of pot still consists of a simple pot with one retort. The latter is a vessel in which a weak alcohol distillate is placed. The vapors from the pot bubble through this distillate and deposit some of the high boiling congeners and water thereby allowing the heat of vaporization to evaporate the alcohol from the distillate in the retort. This product is also considered medium-bodied, unless it is distilled from the type of fermentation used in producing high ester rums.

Pot Distillation Common in Jamaica

The Adams pot still, which consists of a pot with two retorts, is used exclusively in Jamaica and it has become popular in other West Indian islands. It produces the full and medium-bodied rums that characterize the blends made in Jamaica. The first retort contains a distillate known as "low wine," while the second retort contains high wines. The pot is filled with wash containing 7% alcohol and then heated by means of a steam coil, a jacket at the base of the pot, or an external (or internal) calandria. Vapor given off during the first part of the cycle (the rum segment) contains an average of about 25% alcohol. This is bubbled through the liquid in the low wine retort (the liquid contains about 35% alcohol); the water part of the pot still vapor condenses thus releasing heat, which vaporizes the alcohol in the low wine.

The vapor leaving the low wine retort is richer in alcohol than the liquid in the retort. The exit vapor, now containing about 50% alcohol enters the high wine retort, which contains a mixture with about 75% alcohol. Here again, the entering vapor gives up some of its heat of vaporization to evaporate the alcohol in the high wine. The enriched vapor leaving the retort consists of about 85% alcohol and 15% water. This is slightly higher than the concentration achieved by distilling twice in a Scotch malt whisky still. The final vapor is condensed into a distillate called "rum."

As the heating cycle proceeds, the alcoholic content of the condensate begins to decrease, and the rum product is "cut off" when the concentration is reduced to 82%. This rum fraction, with an average strength of 83% alcohol, usually amounts to 7% of the wash charge in the pot. A second fraction is collected between the concentrations of 82 and 70% as high wine. The third fraction, called low wine, is collected until the final distillate contains no alcohol, which signifies that all alcohol has been exhausted from the system. The pot still cycle is now complete after a time lapse of about 5 hours. All the containers are then emptied. The rum is transferred to the bonded warehouse and the high and low wine fractions are pumped to their respective retorts. The pot is again filled with wash and another heating cycle is started.

These percentages are not universal; the cut off strengths may vary depending on the type of rum desired by the distiller. One of the disadvantages of the Adams still is the low efficiency due to the poor contact between the vapor and the liquids in the retorts. It is not as intimate as say, the contact on trays of a continuous still.

Pot-column Hybrid Distillation System

Another effective method of making rum would be to have a pot working in conjunction with a short rectifier. The benefit is better control of the end product and efficiency. The rectifying column may have an internal dephlegmator or external condenser to create reflux thus enhancing the strength of the product. A distiller using this system must take heads, hearts, and tails cuts during the cycle. The hearts may be up to 90% alcohol depending on the reflux ratio and desired flavor. The heads and tails can be returned to the next distillation cycle but they must be eventually discarded to avoid a buildup of undesirable congeners. The system is also ideal for distilling flavorful whiskies, brandy, and for making gin. More will be said about using this system of distillation in the next chapter.

Pot still rums, made from a clean type of fermentation are very similar in congeneric levels to a pot-still malt whisky, rye whisky, or bourbon. This type of rum may even have a similar character to an alambic brandy and it is sometimes difficult to distinguish, on an organoleptic or analytical basis, one distillate from another. This supports the argument that differences in alcoholic beverages are due as much to the method of distillation as to the raw material used in their manufacture.

COLUMN DISTILLATION

Lighter rums are made on a two-column continuous still, which is based on the design principles of the Coffey still. A typical still is identical to that used for distilling other light alcohol beverages. It consists of two columns (the diameter of which depend on the volume to be produced), flow meters, pumps and coolers.

The first column is known as the wash column or analyzer. It is approximately 10 meters(32.8ft) tall with about 25 trays spaced 46cm (1.5ft) apart throughout the height of the column. The spacing is to allow for a man to get into the column in order to remove the calcium scale that periodically builds up in the column. Each tray is perforated and is usually made of copper; they may also be housed in a stainless steel shell which is usually less expensive than copper.

Dead wash, "beer" in whisky parlance, is pumped to the top of the column via a heat exchanger at the top of the analyzer that preheats the wash. Steam, at a pressure of about 7 kg, is injected at the base of the column; this comes into contact with the wash as it falls through the holes in the plates. The steam and wash flows have to be carefully balanced so that a vapor may go up the holes and suspend a layer of wash on each tray. It should be understood that a reduction in steam flow will cause the wash to just fall through the holes and no boiling will take place. By the same token, a drop in the flow rate of wash will result in too much vapor going up through the holes; this will prevent the wash from passing down to the bottom of the column. Carry-over or boil-over of liquid to the condensers or into the vapor going to the rectifier (in the case of the Coffey still) is a problem since cleaning these components is not a simple task.

These flows, steam, and wash are kept in balance by a complex set of flow and pressure recorder/controllers. Each tray acts as a mini-pot still; the vapor leaving the top of the column is used to preheat, in a heat exchanger (beer preheater), the wash that is pumped into the column. This vapor, after condensing in a second heat exchanger, becomes high wine or surge containing about 60% alcohol and 40% water. There is also a vent condenser to vent incondensable gases and separate aldehydes or heads. This system is different from the Coffey still in two respects. In the Coffey still system, the vapor is not condensed since it is fed directly into the rectifier and the wash is heated in a coil that goes through the rectifier whereas in the above, the wash is preheated in the condenser/preheater. Both systems are presently used for making light rums. The liquid leaving the base of the wash column, consisting of water and dead yeast, is known as dunder. When it cools, it has the pungent smell of rotten eggs, which is caused by the putrefaction of the yeast. Some distilleries have tried to recover the yeast but this has never proved to be economical.

The condensed high wine is then fed into the lower part of the rectifier, which is the second column in the system. It is about 12 meters (39.3ft) high with 45 bubble cap or tunnel cap trays spaced 22cm (8.7in) apart. Sieve trays may also be used but these are not as efficient as the latter two. Each tray is fitted with a receptacle on the periphery with a pipeline leading from it to the outside of the column. The various congeners and desired product are removed via these pipelines. The steam that is fed to the column vaporizes the high wine, which consists of the five basic compounds, water (Boiling Point 100°C, 212°F), fusel oils (BP 85°C, 185°F), light rum (BP 82°C, 179.6°F), esters and acids (BP 83°C, 181.4°F), and aldehydes (BP 80°C, 176°F). Some water and fatty acids that never vaporized will collect at the bottom of the column; this should not contain more than 0.2% alcohol. As the vapor minus the water rises up the column, it will find a region where the temperature is around 85°C (185°F), which is the most stable zone in the column and the point at which the fusel oils will condense. A temperature controller inserted in this area can be used to control the flow of product from the column via an automatic valve modulated by the temperature.

This process continues throughout the height of the column, several fractions can be removed at various levels on the column so that rum, relatively free of congeners, is taken off somewhere near the top of the column. The vapor constituents that do not condense on the trays go through a pipe (at the top of the column) to heat exchangers where they are condensed using water as a coolant. The condensate, which contains mainly alcohol and aldehydes, is returned to the column as reflux; this helps to replenish the rum spirit that is removed from the system. A small portion of this return is drawn off so as to prevent the buildup of aldehydes in the product.

The quality or flavor of the product can be altered by allowing fusel oil, esters, and aldehydes to permeate into the product section of the column. This is done by reducing the quantities that are taken out of the column in order to allow one or more of the congeners to build up in the column. This rectifier is again similar to the Coffey rectifier, except for the fact that the feed to the rectifier is a vapor in the case of the Coffey still.

These distillation systems are big users of water both for steam and for cooling. It takes about 5 kg of steam to produce 1 liter of rum in a two-column system where the high wine is fed to the second column as a liquid. However, usage in the Coffey is slightly less since there is no high wine to be re-boiled. The condensing system uses about 35 liters of water for every liter of rum produced. It is desirable to use soft or cooling tower water in the condensers since lime scale in the tubes is difficult to remove. The most effective way of removing scale is to circulate an ortho-phosphoric acid, commercially known by the trade name Lime-A-Way, through the tubes but care must be taken since this will have a corrosive effect on stainless or mild steel.

The Coffey distillation system or the two-column system described above are not designed to make the neutral molasses spirit required for blending with heavier rum or for making molasses based alcohol used in the production of gin, vodka and liqueurs. These products are made on a three-column still. This type of still merely has additional trays so that the congeners are better separated and easier to remove. The alcohol is also produced at a higher strength, i.e. there is less water in the product. Multi-column distillation can be used to produce rum but the system is quite complex. These are usually used to conserve energy in the production of high proof ethanol.

DUNDER

Dunder is the spent liquid left in the still after the rum mash has undergone the primary distillation (beer-stripping). For each liter of rum produced there are up to 16 liters of dunder. In other distilling contexts, dunder is referred to as "backset" when it is used in future batches, or as "residue" when it is simply discarded or used for livestock feed.

The dunder from a previous batch is often used by the distillery in place of some of the water used to dilute the cane sugar for a new batch of rum mash. Dunder contains concentrated rum flavors that can make positive contributions to the profile of future batches. It also helps to acidify the new batch since it has a pH of about 3.3.

Effluent problems in dunder have become a major environmental issue and the high levels of Biochemical Oxygen Demand and Chemical Oxygen Demand (up to 30,000 ppm and 80,000 ppm respectively) must be reduced before the dunder can be discharged into water supplies. Companies that have huge resources can use anaerobic fermentation to produce methane gas but the capital cost required for this does not have an attractive payback. However, methane can be used to supplement about 60% of the oil requirement in running a distillery. Dunder, in countries that have vast areas of cane land, can also be used for ferti-irrigation since it contains many of the nutrients required for cane cultivation. It has also been proposed for melting ice on roadways but it must first be concentrated and mixed with magnesium chloride. This has not been proven to be commercially viable, so common salt is still widely used for the purpose.

FUSEL ALCOHOLS

Higher alcohols, known as fusel oils or fusel alcohols, are insoluble in water and they allow distillers to control the operation of the continuous still as well as contribute to the taste of the rum. The esters formed in a column can be detected throughout the column, and smells of banana and pineapple are easily detected in a rectifier. Esters have almost the same boiling point as ethyl alcohol and are not easily separated. They are very evident in pot still rums.

In analyzing the rum in a lab distillation, low boiling fractions (compounds that have a lower boiling temperature than alcohol) contain aldehydes, second and third fractions contain esters and ethyl alcohol, the fourth fraction contains 65 – 70% of the total fusel oil and the fifth fraction contains high molecular weight oils and fatty acids or "rum oils". It was an old custom to discard the top layer of liquid in a bottle in order to discard the rum oils. This custom and/or shaking the bottle is not required but it does seem that, in the old days of distillation, rum oils may have been abundant. And it is essential to distill rum in copper vessels since the copper reacts with the sulfur compounds formed by the yeast to produce copper sulfide.

— *Chapter Eight* —

BATCH DISTILLATION OF RUM UTILIZING A RECTIFICATION COLUMN

Eric Watson

In prior chapters of this book, the goals of rum distillation and the basic chemistry of the congeneric profiles found in various rums was well covered, so in this chapter I will be focusing on the application of modern equipment that uses a pot still and rectification column in the production of rum.

In most of the regions associated with rum production, there are two methodologies of distillation that are undertaken. The methods are: double distillations utilizing a pot still alone and utilizing stripping columns and continuous columns, most frequently in series. These columns are heated via steam injection and utilize a reverse flow configuration whereby the wash or low wines enter at the top of the column. As the wash flows downward from tray to tray, the alcohol is stripped and rises in the column. This process is very efficient in both energy and output, but is expensive technologically. These types of columns are typically the province of producers desiring a scale of economy that is not often needed or affordable in the craft spirits industry. The use of these columns is only justifiable if your plant has a significant fermentation capacity so that you can use them frequently enough to justify the investment. The type of columns covered below are those used in conjunction with a pot still to achieve more exacting rum attributes as well as distillation to higher proofs.

To many of the individuals entering the craft spirits industry, the allure is the perceived traditional nature of the art of distillation. Unfortunately, blindly adhering to only "traditional" equipment and techniques can sometimes serve to limit what is possible within a distillery. It is always worthwhile to study the traditional methods employed in spirit production but there is also much merit in studying more modern approaches. With the rise of craft spirit production in North America, it is now more common to witness a blend of technologies in batch distillation systems. This is a necessity for most due to the desire to produce multiple products from the same distillation system. This is where the most versatile implementations come into play, combining a pot still with a rectification column (sometimes referred to as a reflux column).

Rum is a congeneric spirit. Even in the most highly rectified rums, which tend to have more in common with vodka than more flavorful rums, there are just enough congeners that result from careful distillation that the resultant spirit can be readily identified as rum. If a batch distillation system is equipped with a rectification column containing enough plates, a distillery can produce the whole spectrum of rums including white or silver rums. Additionally, this same system can be used to produce virtually any other spirit with the exception of vodka from washes. Without a significant number of plates (28+) you cannot rectify the spirit efficiently into a high enough proof and with the expected neutrality to qualify as vodka. You can, however, purchase cane or grain neutral spirits and use these systems to re-distill the spirit into vodka. Even though this is possible, it is not as efficient to use these styles of distillation systems for vodka production if your production needs are large. Often to meet demand the re-distilled spirit is blended into non-redistilled grain neutral spirits to create the final product.

I have specified and used a variety of configurations of distillation systems for rum production. In the Caribbean, we use a former Black Forest schnapps[1] still that was re-configured to include a 6-plate column. This still is particularly unique because it has a bulbous helmet which serves to expand the copper surface area much like the ogee on a whisky still (the small bulb-like shaped bulge typically just above the pot still in the neck) except this one is proportionally larger. The extra surface area and the initial reflux it created made for a unique rum that differs from that produced on the type of system I am about to outline, which is comprised of the more typical cylindrical helmet mounted on top of a pot still. This particular design is capable of producing a very light fractional rum due to it having 9 plates and a pre-condenser.

To produce rum with this system it is best and most efficient to do a double distillation. The typical rum wash contains between 7% and 8% alcohol by volume. This is the range of alcohol production that produces

---

1 German schnapps is a fruit brandy, not the sweet liqueur North Americans call "schnapps."

the best flavor profiles in rums. This wash is pumped into the pot still and a quick distillation is undertaken to remove the alcohol and congeners from the wash. The first distillation is called a stripping run and it produces low wines and no cuts are taken at this stage. On average, this distillation step takes 3-5 hours and results in low wines with an alcohol content between 35% and 45% by volume.

To set the distillation system up for low wine production, the rectification column is bypassed allowing the vapor exiting the pot still to go directly to the spirit condenser. In the illustration below this bypass is not depicted, but is attached as needed by disconnecting the elbows that angle down from the pot still discharge into the column and the one serving the top of the spirit condenser. These elbows are then spun and a bridge pipe is inserted connecting the pot still discharge to the top of the spirit condenser.

Once the bypass has been established, the wash is heated to a rolling boil and is distilled until the output of the condenser is at the same alcohol level as was present in the wash.

Going beyond this point requires a disproportionate amount of energy to yield any significant amount of alcohol and the quality of this alcohol is greatly diminished over that initially distilled. This energy increase occurs because of the higher water content and the increasing difficulty of separating the alcohol from it.

The second distillation, known as a spirit run, utilizes both the pot still and the rectification column, so the bypass is eliminated by re-connecting the piping supplying the column. The low wines are typically diluted (if required) to 35% to 40% alcohol by volume to enhance the amount of time the vapors are in contact with the copper surfaces. This alcohol range is not a hard and fast rule. Due to variations in the way distilling systems are manufactured, it is best to try varying dilutions to see what results in the best profiles. With the distillation system I use in the Caribbean, the best results were obtained when the pre-spirit run low wines were proofed to 38% abv. However, with the system depicted in this chapter, low wines with a higher proof can be used due to the additional plates and the size of the column.

When undertaking a spirit run, the boil rate should be just at a simmer so that the distillation can take place gently. This allows for better separation of the heads, hearts and tails cuts.

Table I illustrates a distillation system comprised of a pot still with a cylindrical helmet, a pre-condenser, a 9-plate column equipped with bubble caps and a spirit condenser. Some manufacturers like to differentiate their systems by calling the pre-condenser a "dephlegmator" or other names, but they all produce the same result which is to create reflux within the column.

The distillation system depicted has some features that may or may not be required or desirable to every distillery's needs. I have included these items to illustrate the maximum implementation (other than automation) so that the reader can be acquainted with these capabilities should the need arise. The two depicted items that can be optional are the agitator and the dual stage condenser.

Agitators are desirable for a number of reasons and necessary in others. When you are distilling from a wash that contains a high amount of solids, agitators allow for better distillation performance and eliminate hot spots that can scorch washes. I believe that agitation is mandatory under this scenario. The desirable aspect of agitation, but not a requirement, is enhanced heating performance since the whole wash comes in contact with the heating surfaces at all times. Additionally, if your pot still utilizes an internal steam coil or colandria instead of the depicted low pressure steam jacket, it is best to use agitation to reduce fowling of the heating surfaces which can be difficult to clean. I have not mentioned using electricity as a heating method as it should only be used where no other solution is available. Electric stills are indirectly heated by a water bath that jackets the lower 1/2 to 1/3 of the still body. The only advantage to this method is first-time installation cost. Unfortunately this "saving" is rapidly erased by utility costs. Additionally, they can be harder to control as they usually are installed with discrete stages that energize and de-energize the electric coils. If there are not enough stages and/or the control system is not set up properly, distillation performance can suffer.

The dual-stage condenser depicted is actually a design that I used in the Caribbean. Its inclusion was mandatory because the average incoming water temperature there is above 80 degrees year around. Efficiently condensing spirits requires an entering water temperature of 60°-65°F (15.5°-18.3°C). In the depicted example, the first stage of the condenser (at the top) is cooled with domestic water and the second stage is cooled with a glycol and water solution.

There are many regions in the South and Southwest in the United States that have higher than desirable water temperatures. Another way I have successfully met this challenge is to install a small plate and frame heat exchanger in the supply line for the condenser. The water is cooled

TABLE I

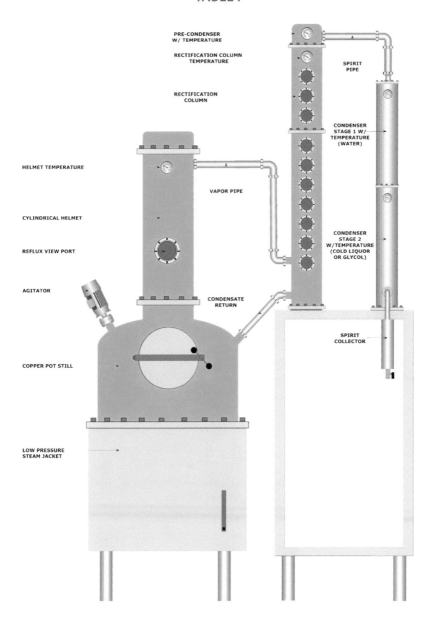

PRE-CONDENSER
W/ TEMPERATURE

RECTIFICATION COLUMN
TEMPERATURE

SPIRIT
PIPE

RECTIFICATION
COLUMN

CONDENSER
STAGE 1 W/
TEMPERATURE
(WATER)

HELMET TEMPERATURE

VAPOR PIPE

CYLINDRICAL HELMET

REFLUX VIEW PORT

CONDENSER
STAGE 2
W/TEMPERATURE
(COLD LIQUOR
OR GLYCOL)

AGITATOR

CONDENSATE
RETURN

COPPER POT STILL

SPIRIT
COLLECTOR

LOW PRESSURE
STEAM JACKET

down to the appropriate range via a glycol loop within the heat exchanger. This implementation tends to be cheaper than a dual stage condenser and also utilizes a resource that most distilleries already or should have… the glycol or cold water (aka Cold Liquor) that is used to control fermentation temperatures.

An additional benefit to condensing spirit in this temperature range is that gauging becomes more accurate. This is due to the fact that hydrometers are calibrated to 60°F (15.5°C). The closer to this temperature the sample is, the more accurate hydrometers are. Any deviation from 60°F (15.5°C) requires the use of a correction table to closer approximate the actual alcohol level.

Table II illustrates the internals of the rectification column serving the depicted distillation system. The dashed red lines represent the vapors that are rising through the column and the solid blue lines represent condensed vapors that are working their way back to the pot still to be redistilled. This column is supplied with single large "bubble caps" that serve each plate. These caps serve as an additional surface area upon which the vapors can condense and form a layer of liquid on the plate, comprised of water, oils and other congeners. This helps to further refine the spirit since the vapors that rise beyond the plate are forced through the accumulated liquid.

Above a certain level, weir or "weep" drains allow excessive liquid to drain downwards back into the well at the bottom of the column which drains back into the pot still via piping situated above the liquid level in the still. In some column designs, "switches" are added that allow the plugging of the weir drains to more finely control the water accumulation on the plates. Depending on the desires of the operator, some or all of these switches might be used to produce differing results.

The amount of reflux or returning spirit and water is controlled by the pre-condenser. The pre-condenser and the remaining plates serving the depicted still are illustrated in Table III. In this example, cold water is introduced into an internal coil at the top of the column. The rate of water flow is controlled by an automatic thermostatic control valve. The higher the flow rate, the colder the coil becomes and creates greater reflux which results in a higher exiting proof into the condenser. Using this method of operation is easier than trying to control the reflux by varying the temperature in the pot still because achieving fine steam control is difficult with manual steam valves. With a pre-condenser you can simply boil the pot still contents and finely control the reflux by the water flow to the

TABLE II

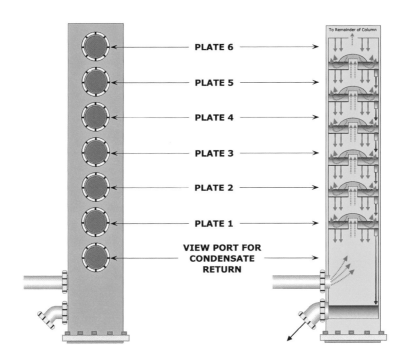

TABLE III

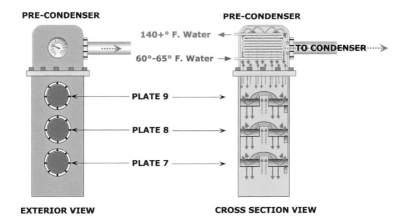

pre-condenser, achieving greater accuracy, efficiency, and usually, results. There are a number of other pre-condenser designs that vary from what is simply a water bucket with piping to the depicted coil. Coil designs tend to use less water than other designs.

The use of columns in distillation allows for a more concentrated heads cut being collected which results in a greater volume of hearts. This is achieved by what I term "column stacking." This is the concentration of low-boiling-point compounds that are detrimental to the spirit profile and in some cases are also toxic and/or have carcinogenic properties. Most notable among these are methanol and ethyl-carbamate. The latter is coming under greater scrutiny and presently in Europe it is strictly monitored. It is only a matter of time until all countries will have established maximum thresholds for that compound.

To create column stacking, a high degree of cooling water is applied to the pre-condenser so that the majority of the vapor in the column is condensed and allowed to run back to the pot still. The vapor that does not condense remains "stacked" in the upper reaches of the column because it is too cold for them to continue into the spirit condenser. The column is held in this state for 30 minutes or slightly longer to concentrate what will become the heads fraction. After a sufficient amount of time has elapsed, the water flow is slowly reduced so that the heads begin to run into the condenser allowing for them to be separated out.

Chapter 9

MATURATION, BLENDING & VATTING

MATURATION

Before beginning this section, it is important to address a topic that has recently proven a difficult challenge for craft distillers. The word age refers to a number. The word maturation refers to a flavor. If you are already in the industry, you no doubt have had the question from consumers: "how old is it." Since the late '60s, consumers have been marketed to so that they are convinced that older age equates with better flavor. Many bar owners are also perpetuating this, no doubt to the benefit of their pockets as well! Since most craft spirits are young in comparison to those from longer established producers, if you answer that question directly with "4 months" or something similar, you may have to defend the youth of your product to overcome resistance. Instead, we should all use the words mature and maturation in place of age and aging. This will allow us the opportunity to discuss the flavors we are targeting as producers.... something a consumer can immediately quantify when tasting your spirits!

The maturation of spirits is a complex set of chemical interactions made deceptively simple by allowing new spirits to sit in white oak barrels. Maturation is the process by which alcohols, esters, and oils present in the spirit oxidize and interact with the chemical components of the oak barrel to form new compounds that add color, flavor, and body to the spirit. The rate of maturation is dependent on a number of factors including: barrel size, smaller barrels have a higher ratio of surface area to volume; temperature fluctuations, larger temperature swings in the aging warehouse causes the spirit to expand into and out of the barrel more rapidly, speeding up the maturation process; humidity, high humidity causes barrels to exhale ethanol, while low humidity causes barrels to exhale water; and atmospheric pressure, which is less understood but seems to play a role.

Rum fresh off the still can be raw and harsh to the taste so it is common practice to warehouse and mature the rum for a number of years, often in 180 liter (47.5 gallon) oak casks or large wooden vats. The casks are usually once-used charred American bourbon barrels. The average maturation time for rum is usually about one to two years though it is not uncommon to find rums aged for 10 years or more. These older rums are sold at a premium price due to the losses incurred by evaporation. The amount of loss due to evaporation depends on a number of environmental factors in the aging warehoused like heat, humidity and atmospheric pressure. None the less some amount of rum vapor will pass through the pores of the wood and expand as it leaves, often creating a pleasant smell in the aging warehouse. Rums in the tropics age quite quickly when compared to spirits aged in cooler climes. For instance, some West Indian rums are sent to the U.K. for aging and a 30 year old rum in that country may have a similar character as the same rum aged for 10 years in the tropics.

Barrels can be used more than once but the life of a barrel is somewhat less in a tropical climate than in a temperate climate where a barrel may last up to 80 years with several turns. Three turns are normal and the barrel once exhausted may be used as firewood, a planter or for barbecue chips. Swishing the barrel, adding water to a recently emptied barrel to extract more alcohol from the wood, is illegal in some counties but the practice does exist, especially in North America and most likely Scotland.

Rum, like any other new distillate is colorless but as it matures it takes on a pale amber hue from the oak. Some white rums have been aged for a few years to round out some of the harsh edges of the new distillate and then charcoal filtered to remove their color. However, many white rums are sold un-aged, so it is not necessary to carbon treat these brands to remove the barrel color.

The labeling requirements for the age of rum vary from country to country. The US does not require rum to bear a statement of age but if it does, the age must represent the youngest rum in the product. Rums produced in the West Indies with a declared age should abide by the Scottish and Canadian protocol where the declaration indicates the time spent in the barrel. However, there are countries that use an average age system. In this case a bottle with 10 and 4 year old rums could be declared as 7 years old irrespective of how much of each are in the blend. It can be an arithmetic mean rather than a weighted average. Some countries call this a Solera system. A test for age is to allow the rum to evaporate, the sediment left after a few days will indicate the deposits from the barrel, this assumes however, that the rum was not filtered and no other solids were added to it.

Blending & Vatting

It is important to understand the distinction between blending and vatting. Blending is colloquially used as a synonym for vatting but there is a technical difference. Vatting is when a distillery mixes different batches of their own products that are all of the same libation as the stated spirit. On the other hand, blending is when spirits from different manufacturers are mixed together to form the stated spirit product. And, blended spirits can include grain neutral spirits and other special-purpose distillates and infusions that may not be of the same type of libation as the stated spirit.

Most of the rum produced in the West Indies is sold to other countries that buy the full-bodied rums in bulk and blend them with locally produced molasses spirit. As described in chapter one, this is common practice in Canada and Germany. The versatility of rum also has made it popular as a base for fruit-flavored blends such as coconut rum, pineapple rum, and other liqueurs. There is however, a large output of branded bottled rums especially in Jamaica that are not blended, but vatted.

Vatted rums can be white, colored, aged, or unaged, and they are often derived from a mixture of pot and continuous distillates. Vatting allows distillers to mix various batches of their products to achieve consistency without having to label their products as "blended." Vatting also allows distillers to create a different version of the same product. For example, Scottish malt whisky distilleries vat their scotches for consistency, and to create different versions of their whisky. A given distillery might vat their single-malt scotch to produce a 12-year-old, a 16-year-old, and a 21-year-old version of their same stated product. In this way, "vatting" is not "blending" and the distillery can still claim their product to be "single malt" because the Scotch only consists of malt whisky made at one distillery. For our purposes the blender and blend they create refers to a vatted mix of rums all produced at a single distillery.

When vatting rum, the blender typically selects and examines the available rum prior to making up the final blend. Since there are many types of rum, aged, unaged, full-bodied, light-bodied etc., a brand is usually made up of many different components and blending becomes a very skillful art. Once a formula is arrived at that matches the desired flavor and body profile, the blender selects his or her casks and does a pre-blend in large wooden or stainless steel vats. The rums are left to "marry" and then vatted again to ensure continuity of the finished product. After an adequate marrying time, the vatted rum is reduced with demineralized or reverse osmosis water and rested prior to filtration and bottling. Because of this process, rum can produce an infinite variety of blends and there are more variations of rum than any other alcoholic beverage. So experiment and find the profiles that match your vision.

Chapter 10

EXAMPLE RECIPE FOR AMBER RUM

Ian Smiley

The following is a recipe for a medium-bodied amber rum made entirely from Grade A molasses. Starting with 5 barrels (5 bbls = 155 gallons) of mash, it should yield about 11 gallons of 70 - 75% rum. The rum will be distilled twice in a whiskey-style pot still, aged for two years in a 25-gallon barrel coopered from used bourbon-barrel staves. After two years the rum can be proofed, vatted, color adjusted with the addition of some cane spirit caramel, filtered, and bottled.

After tasting the rum from this batch, the distiller can determine if (s)he wants to increase or decrease the intensity of the rum flavor. The flavor can be lightened by using white sugar or intensified by using blackstrap molasses. By switching to a different grade of molasses, blending two or more grades of molasses, and/or adding white sugar the distiller can formulate a rum recipe right for them.

Ingredients

130 gal Warm mash water (around 95°F, 35°C)

10 gal Dunder (if available, just use additional mash water if not)

265 lbs Grade A molasses (i.e. good quality table molasses)

6.5 oz Go Ferm® by Lallemand

5 oz Diammonium Phosphate (DAP)

5 oz Fermaid K® by Lallemand

5 oz Suitable yeast for rum fermentation selected from the strains of dried yeast named in the Yeast Section in Chapter 4, "Raw Ingredients."

Equipment

175 – 200 gal open stainless-steel tote to serve as a fermentor

175 – 200 gal pot still as used for whiskey or brandy

Plate filter with 1-Micron filters

Fermentation

Place the molasses and the DAP in the tote fermentor. Add 10 gal of dunder and 70 gal of warm mash water and mix thoroughly to dissolve the molasses and DAP. Fill up the fermentor with water to 155 gal (5 bbls). The SG should be about 1.070 (17.1 Brix).

In a separate container (at least 3-4 gallons in size) mix the Go Ferm® in 1 gallon of warm mash water (110°F, 43.3°C) and mix thoroughly to dissolve. Once this nutrient solution has cooled to 104°F (40°C), add the dried yeast to the nutrient solution and stir gently to break any clumps. Let the suspension stand for 15-30 minutes and then gently stir again. Live yeast populations decline when allowed to stand for more than 30 minutes.

Then, over a period of 5 minutes, slowly combine an equal amount (1 gallon) of the main molasses mash to the yeast suspension. This is called "attemperation" and will help the yeast adjust to the cooler temperature of the mash when they are combined and avoid cold shocking the yeast. A rapid temperature drop exceeding a delta of 18°F can traumatize the yeast and cause a slow fermentation. If the temperature drop from the 104°F yeast suspension to the temperature of the main mash is more than 18°F (unlikely to be the case with a rum mash), then a second attemperation step would have to be carried out by the addition of another gallon of the main mash over a period of 5 minutes.

Ensure the temperature of the mash is under 100°F (37.8°C) and mix in the 2 gallons of yeast suspension mash mixture. If the fermentor has a cover, keep it lightly covered so the CO_2 pressure can escape. Some distilleries just leave the fermentors open at the top. The liquid temperature should be controlled to stay between 80-90°F (26.7-32.2°C).

After about 1/3 of the sugar in the mash has been depleted, add the Fermaid K®. With an Original Gravity of 1.070, this would be when the SG has dropped to about 1.045. This is not likely to take more than about 24 hours. With the aforementioned nutrient regimen, the fermentation should take about 3 days. If only the DAP is used, then fermentation will take more like 5 or 6 days. The SG at the end of fermentation should be about 1.005.

First Distillation: Stripping Run

Siphon the liquid off the sediment into the pot still for the first distillation (i.e. the beer-stripping run). For the beer-stripping, there will be no separation of heads, hearts, and tails. The distillation will simply run until the total distillate received (i.e. low wines) is down to 35% abv. There will be very little alcohol coming out of the still by the time the low wines are at 35% abv.

Second Distillation: Spirit Run

Clean the still out thoroughly, and place the low wines back in the still for the spirit run (second run). Heat the still to the level suitable for running off an aromatic spirit. When the distillate begins to run, receive the first spirit into a receiver labeled "Heads." For a 5-bbl batch size there will be roughly 1.6 gallons of heads. Begin smelling and tasting the spirit right away, and when the solvent-like smell and taste subside and the spirit just tastes of an intense rum flavor, switch to the hearts receiver. This is the beginning-cut and the run is now in the "hearts" phase. This begin-cut will take place when the incoming spirit is around 85% abv and when the head temperature is at about 186°F (85.6°C). This temperature could vary slightly depending on the pot still.

Continue to smell and taste the spirit periodically as it is flowing from the still during the hearts phase, and monitor the still-head temperature. As the temperature rises above 194°F (90°C), watch for taste changes in the flavor of the spirit. Towards the end of the hearts phase, the spirit will start losing its sweetness and begin taking on a grainy, unpleasant flavor. This is the point in the run when the end-cut to the tails phase is made. Switch to a receiver labeled "Tails." The end-cut will take place when the incoming spirit is at about 65% abv, and the head temperature is around 198-200°F (92.2-93.3°C). The Hearts receiver should have about 11 or 12 gallons of rum between 70 and 75% abv.

Run the tails until the abv of the incoming spirit is showing almost no alcohol. The head temperature will be close to 212°F (100°C), and the total alcohol content of the tails will be about 35% abv. For the 5-bbl batch size there will be about 8 gallons of tails. The tails can be saved and used in future batches, so it is wise to end the run when the total alcohol of the tails is down to about 35% abv. Because, even though there is still a little alcohol left in the boiler, the energy needed to extract what little remains is past the point of diminishing returns.

The tails can be mixed with the heads and labeled "Feints." The feints can be cycled through future spirit runs at a rate of approximately 15% feints to 85% new low wine. The rest of the feints should be removed from the rum-making cycle and rectified into pure ethanol for other uses. To continually recycle feints would result in a build-up of unwanted congeners that would eventually make the rum produced undrinkable. So, as the feints-recycling process is established it is important that the excess feints are routinely removed from the cycle and sent for rectifying.

The following table shows the results of a spirit run (second distillation) from a 5-bbl batch of rum mash.

Phase	Amount	Temperature at the time of cut	%Ethanol of incoming spirit at cut	%Ethanol of total Phase
Heads	1.6 gal	186°F / 85.6°C	83% begin-cut	84% abv
Hearts	11 gal	198°F / 92.2°C	65% end-cut	75% abv
Tails	8 gal	212°F / 100°C	3% end-run	35% abv

Barrel Aging

Given that the barrel we have chosen to age the rum in is 25 gallons, it will be necessary to repeat this recipe three times so as to accumulate an ample enough quantity of rum to completely fill the barrel with a considerable amount left over. Incidentally, one can collect all the low wines from three stripping runs and then run them altogether in a single spirit run. The still will easily hold the low wines from three stripping runs.

Make sure the barrel is tight and not leaking by keeping it full of water for two or three days before filling it with rum. In the mean time, the new-make rum should be proofed down to barrel strength, between 65% and 55% abv, with mineral water or pure water. Once the barrel has been swollen out and is not leaking, empty the water out and fill the barrel right up as full as possible with barrel-strength rum and then hammer in a bung. It is best to use a bung that can be removed and replaced as opposed to a bung that must be destroyed in order to remove it. This will aid in periodic sampling during the aging process. Place the barrel in a warm or hot place (up to 100°F, 37.8°C), to age for two years.

Rotate the barrel about an eighth of turn every month or so, and give the barrel a good shake as often as you can. During the aging period, if you see the barrel getting wet anywhere on the outside due to a minor seepage between the staves, take a half-inch chisel and hammer a fairly deep slit about three-eighths of an inch from the leak in each of the two staves beside the leaking seam. Then hammer a cedar wedge into each chisel slit. The cedar wedges can be made by taking a cedar shim and cutting pieces of the wedge to fit the slits. This will tighten the seam between the two staves and stop it from leaking.

The rum should be sampled every month or so. If the barrel has a removable bung, the bung can be removed and a small sample of the rum can be retrieved using a glass or stainless-steel wine thief. Some wine thieves are made of acrylic and they must never be used with distilled spirits. The sample should be deposited in a wine glass or a brandy snifter and an equal amount of water added and swirled to mix it in. Carefully nose and sip the sample to determine the development of its flavor and aroma (bouquet). When the rum has a perfectly balanced flavor, the harshness of the raw rum flavor is gone, and the flavor of the wood and char has mellowed out, the rum is ready for bottling. However, the rum will continue to improve with additional aging, but it is important to make sure the rum is not "going over the top." That is to say, the flavor has not begun to take on too much wood character or become too mellow to the point of becoming insipid, or become unbalanced for other reasons. This is one of the reasons it is important to do periodic samplings.

If the barrel does not have a removable bung, little wooden plugs can be purchased so the person tending to the cellar can drill a given sized hole in the barrel head to let a sample out into a glass, and then the little plug can be hammered into the hole to seal it up again. Many larger commercial distilleries use this method of sampling barrels, but for a smaller-scale operation it is better to use removable bungs.

Bottling

After the rum is aged and has been sampled and approved for bottling, it will be necessary to:
- proof the rum (i.e. dilute it to its precise bottling strength)
- do any blending with other rums
- make an addition of cane spirit caramel
- filter it through a plate filter
- bottle it

First, empty the rum from the barrel into a blending tank. Add enough pure water (demineralized or distilled) to dilute the rum to the desired bottling strength (e.g. 40% abv). Liquor regulating authorities allow for a variation of ±0.2% abv, so be sure to dilute to the top of this allowance (i.e. 40.2% abv). This allows for trace losses in percent alcohol throughout the handling processes up to putting the enclosures on the bottles.

After the rum has been proofed, if there are any other rums to be blended with this one they should be added next. Be sure to proof the other rums before blending them with this one. All rums going into a blend should be at exactly the same percent alcohol.

Cane spirit caramel is added next. Even if the rum formulation does not call for an addition of caramel flavor, most distilleries do add a small amount to adjust the color and hue to a consistent standard for the particular product. Cane spirit caramel should be added in small amounts and sampled until the desired hue is attained. The rum should be mixed thoroughly after each addition of cane spirit caramel to ensure that it is completely dissolved and mixed in.

Finally, the rum is filtered using a plate filter set up with 1-Micron filter pads. This must be the final step before the rum goes into the reservoir of the bottle filler.

After the rum has been bottled, like all spirits and wines, the taste and aroma of the product will not be at its best immediately after bottling. This is often referred to as "bottle shock" or "bottle sickness." It can take the better part of three months for the bottled product to develop its bouquet and for the flavor to mellow out and become balanced.

PART THREE

Rum Resources

What follows is a description of some of today's common rum styles, their commercial expressions, and some thoughts about how craft distillers can contribute to these styles. While not exhaustive, our hope is to identify a few styles in which craft rum could shine.

Chapter 11

RUM STYLES

Martin Cate & Eric Zandona

Once upon a time the world of rum was fairly simple to describe. There were English, Spanish, and French style rums. Rums made in the former British colonies (Jamaica, Barbados, Trinidad, and Guyana among others) were known for producing full-bodied, molasses-based pot distilled rums that were highly aromatic and flavorful. Rums made in former Spanish colonies such as Cuba, Puerto Rico, Nicaragua, and the Dominican Republic, were known for light-bodied, molasses-based rums that were either produced with column stills or distilled multiple times on a pot still. Rums made in the French West Indian islands of Martinique and Guadeloupe became known for a style called Rhum Agricole, a densely aromatic and flavorful rum made from fresh pressed sugar cane juice.

During Prohibition, thirsty American travelers rediscovered rum and fell in love with the light Spanish style rums of Cuba. Since then, the American rum market has been dominated largely by light-bodied rums. This lighter style became so popular that Jamaica and other producers of full-bodied pot distilled rum felt pressure to change in order to survive. They began producing medium-bodied rums made from blending pot and column distillates. In the 1980s, spiced and flavored rums entered the US market and became popular, particularly with younger drinkers. Though infusing rum with spices has had a long tradition throughout the Caribbean, spiced rums did not become a fixture in the US rum market until the launch of Captain Morgan. In the last five to ten years, the cocktail renaissance has sent bartenders and mixologists looking for bolder, more full-bodied rums that offer a wider flavor palette. They want the rum to play a more significant role in the flavor of their cocktails, working in concert with fresh squeezed juices and herb infused syrups to create a layered drink experience that continues to develop from start to finish.

Any attempt to narrowly classify rums today into the old colonial styles quickly breaks down for a couple of reasons. First, the molasses used by most producers is a bulk commodity that is often blended from several countries and contains no discernible traces of terroir, unlike rums made from fresh pressed sugar cane juice. Second, the broad definition of rum makes it possible to find a large variety of "styles" in the current marketplace. Light, dark, amber, gold, black, navy, premium, añejo, spiced, and flavored rums, are almost all based on various blends of light and medium-bodied rums distilled from a molasses wash and aged for varying lengths of time. Third, Rhum Agricole is no longer the only style bound by a geographic location. A few years ago, Venezuela introduced a label of origin for rums produced there. This variety in classification, combined with the resurgence of a spirit and cocktail culture in the Unites States, presents a number of opportunities for craft rum distillers.

What follows is a description of some of today's common rum styles, their commercial expressions, and some thoughts about how craft distillers can contribute to these styles. While not exhaustive, our hope is to identify a few styles in which craft rum could shine.

WHITE RUM

One of the most significant innovations in the rum world was Facundo Bacardi's approach to white rum. Bacardi produced a highly rectified spirit that was aged in oak for a few years and then charcoal filtered to remove the color. The result was light tasting clear rum that had the harsh edges, typical of unaged molasses rum, smoothed out from its time spent in the barrel. Flor de Caña Extra Dry White Rum, and Bacardi Superior are two commercial examples of this style that are widely available.

Craft rum distillers can use the fact that most white rums in the US market follow the Bacardi model to their advantage. There are only a handful of distillers making high quality, full-bodied white rums that have enough flavor and interesting aromatics to be enjoyed on their own or in a well-crafted cocktail. With room to grow in this segment of the market, craft distillers can help expand the conception of white rum beyond a cheap party spirit to include artisanal expressions worthy of a premium price point.

BLACK RUM

Commonly found in Tiki drinks, black rums tend to be opaque and slightly sweet on the tongue, with molasses and burnt caramel flavors.

This style is often briefly aged and darkened with cane spirit caramel. Producing black rum could be good for craft distillers for a couple of reasons. First, the significant addition of caramel to achieve the black opaqueness common to this style can be kind to younger rums. The decision to age rum can be a considerable investment for a craft distiller, so making a black rum could be a good strategy to get a younger spirit to market. Second, craft distillers making a medium to full-bodied rum with notes of ripe banana (amyl acetate) or other fruity esters might find the addition of caramel a good match to their rum's flavor profile.

Spiced Rum

While spiced rum became a fixture of the US rum market after the launch of Captain Morgan, it has experienced its most dramatic growth since the release of Sailor Jerry Spiced Rum and its popularity is likely to continue. The common denominator for all the major spiced rums currently on the market is the fact that they are using concentrated extracts to flavor their products. There are only half a dozen or so distillers who are using real sticks of cinnamon, real vanilla pods, and other spices to infuse their rums with flavor. Craft distillers gained a foothold in the vodka market by using whole pieces of fruit to infuse flavor into their products while larger brands relied on flavor extracts. So too, craft distillers who infuse their rum with real spices can make space for themselves in this very popular segment of the market. Finally, like black rums, spiced rums offer craft distillers an avenue to begin selling relatively young rum while portions of their rum stock continue to age.

Rhum Agricole

In the seventeenth century the French West Indies operated much like the Spanish or British islands. They grew sugar cane as their primary agricultural product, refined the juice into granulated sugar for export and made rum from the leftover molasses. However, in the 1800s this changed. The French decided to stop buying sugar from the West Indies and source it instead from European grown sugar beets. This left the French Caribbean islands with large sugar cane fields and no market for their sugar. In response, the French islands of Martinique, Guadeloupe and others began producing rum directly from fresh pressed sugar cane juice rather than molasses in a distinctive style called Rhum Agricole. Unlike rum made from molasses, rhum agricole contains the distinctive influence of terroir, such that the soil quality, climatic conditions, and availability of water all play a role in the final flavor of the rum. Rhum agricole, when made according to particular style and production standards from specific regions in Martinique, was, until recently, the only rum style to have an AOC (appellation d'origine contrôlée) designation.

Until recently the only available examples of the agricole style of rum in the US were rums produced in the French Caribbean, such as Neisson Rhum or Rhum J.M. However, for the last few years, St. George Spirits in Alameda, California has been producing two agricole-style rums made from fresh pressed sugar cane, grown in the Imperial Valley of California.

For craft distillers, agricole-style rum provides interesting challenges and opportunities. The primary challenge with agricole is the brief window of time between the cane harvest and the start of primary fermentation. Ideally a distillery needs to be able to get the fresh cut cane pressed and into their fermenters within 24 hours. Otherwise, wild yeasts living on the sugar cane will begin fermenting the sugars and produce undesirable flavors in the resulting mash and distillate. St. George has demonstrated that with a bit of coordination it is possible to produce an agricole-style rum. Therefore, distillers that can find or partner with a nearby sugar cane farmer (ideally within a 24 hour drive) have an opportunity to make their own version of an agricole-style rum. And if the cane comes from the distillery's home state their product can capitalize on drinkers' interest in consuming and supporting spirits made from locally grown crops.

Barrel Aged Rums

Fine, barrel aged rums have risen in prestige and taken their place alongside well-aged Scotches and Cognacs. While there are a number of methods to mellow newly distilled rum, barrel aging is still the best method to create a complex and captivating spirit. Don Q Añejo and Appleton Estate Reserve are two examples of well-aged rums. The former is a blend of light-bodied rums aged between three to five years while the latter is a medium-bodied blend of aged pot and column distillates.

In the same way that high quality, aged craft whiskey has found a receptive and thirsty audience, so too will well made, barrel aged craft rum. Tying up inventory in barrels for a number of years can be a significant investment for craft distilleries. But once a good stock of lighter and heavier craft rums come of age it is also likely that distillers will find an enthusiastic public.

SINGLE BARREL RUM

Single barrel rum simply refers to an aged rum that has been bottled completely from one barrel. While it is common to find single barrel bottlings produced by distillers of single malt whiskies, it is less common to find single barrel rum bottlings. The most widely available single barrel rum in the US market today is Cruzan Single Barrel Estate Rum. Cruzan first vats a selection of their aged rums and then finishes this mixture in charred new oak barrels for six to nine months. Each barrel is then individually proofed down to 40% abv and bottled. Because each barrel matures the rum slightly differently than the one next to it, single barrel bottlings do not have the same consistency as other products. But for many drinkers these differences are part of the appeal.

Here again craft distillers have an opportunity. It has become common to see craft whiskeys numbered in some way to indicate they were bottled one barrel at a time. This same kind of paradigm can be carried over into the bottling of craft rum. Craft distillers that produce bourbon, or some other type of whiskey that requires aging in a charred new oak barrels, can reuse these barrels to age their rum. Doing so can be an added selling point for the rum's flavor development, especially if it is released in single barrel bottlings.

SINGLE VINTAGE RUM

The term "single vintage rums" refers to aged rums that were produced in a single calendar year. One of the only rums that is made in this style comes from Plantation Rum, a label owned by the same people who produce Cognac Ferrand and Citadelle Gin. They buy a variety of aged rums from a single country that were distilled the same year, blend them and age them in France in French oak casks. Recent bottlings in their vintage series include Plantation Jamaica 2000, Plantation Trinidad 1999, and Plantation Grenada 2003.

For craft distillers offering a vintage bottling of rum could be good for a couple of reasons. First, a vintage offering builds in the expectation that the current vintage is different than last year's vintage. For distillers still trying to work out a rum profile that they want to produce all the time, vintage bottlings give them the opportunity to sell their product without committing to a particular profile. Also, for any distiller that decides to make an Agricole-style rum, the vintage could refer to the year of the cane harvest.

SOLERA RUM

The solera system of aging wine and spirits was first implemented by Spanish sherry producers and adopted by a small number of rum producers in Latin America. The solera method of ageing in its simplest form is a system of fractional blending where only some portion of an older blend (usually one-third to one-half) is bottled and a slightly younger spirit is used to refill the older barrel. One of the most common rums in this style, Ron Zacapa Centenario 23 Solera Rum, is a blend of rums aged between six and twenty-three years in used whiskey and sherry barrels. To accomplish this task Zacapa has a very large aging facility and computerized tracking to stay on top of their complicated system. The result, however, is a highly awarded spirit. One side note, Zacapa claims that their use of sugar cane honey, the first sugar syrup concentration produced from cane juice, is part of what makes their rum unique.

The idea of using a solera method for aging crafts spirits is slowly gaining traction, though the only bottling currently available as of this writing is Hillrock Estate Distillery's Solera Aged Bourbon. Distillers who produce one or more varieties of rum and have the room to mature their rum in this way may find a very receptive market for a craft solera rum.

There are a number of other rum styles not discussed here that craft distillers have had success with. The wide variety of rum styles and broad parameters of each lend themselves to the creativity of the craft movement. This diversity of rum styles allows distillers the opportunity to create a product that matches personality, values and production capacity.

Chapter 12

REINVENTING CLASSIC RUM COCKTAILS

One common marketing strategy is to develop a signature cocktail that highlights the best attributes of your product. Modifying a classic cocktail has the advantages of being immediately recognizable as well as easy for your customers to order and easy for bartenders to make. Below are ten classic rum cocktails that can be experimented with and morphed into a drink that can help make your brand better known.

Rum and Cola

2oz Rum
4oz Cola (preferably one sweetened with sugar cane)
1oz of Lime Juice (for a Cuba Libre)
In a glass with ice mix all ingredients and stir. Garnish with lime wedge.

Mojito

2oz White Rum
1oz Fresh lime juice
10 Mint Leaves
.75oz simple syrup
Soda water
Muddle mint with sugar and lime juice. Add ice and rum, top with soda water. Garnish with sprig of mint leaves. Serve with straw.

Hurricane

1oz Light Rum
1oz Dark Rum
OJ and Pineapple juice
.5oz Grenadine
Float .5oz 151 rum

Egg Nog
.75oz Brandy
.75oz Rum
.5oz Sugar
3oz Whole Milk or Heavy Cream
1 Whole Egg
Thoroughly mix all ingredients in a shaker with ice.
Strain into a glass and garnish with nutmeg.

Daiquiri
2 oz Rum
.75 oz Lime Juice
1tsp Sugar
Shake ingredients with ice and strain into a chilled cocktail glass.

Mai Tai
2oz light Rum
.5oz Triple Sec
.5oz Grenadine
Fill with OJ and Pineapple juice
Float .5oz Dark Rum
In a glass filled with ice add first three liquors
and top off with fruit juice.
Float a dark rum and garnish with a straw, and or a slice of fruit.

Piña Colada
1oz Rum
1oz Coconut Cream or Milk
3oz Pineapple Juice
Blend or shake with crushed ice until smooth.
Garnish with pineapple wedge and maraschino cherry and straw.

Zombie
1oz Light Rum
.5oz Grenadine
.5oz Triple Sec
Pineapple Juice and Orange Juice
Float .5oz 151 rum
In a glass filled with ice add first three liquors and top off with fruit

juice. Float 151 rum and garnish with a straw, maraschino cherry and or a slice of fruit.

Planters Punch
2oz Dark Rum
1oz Fresh lemon juice
.3oz Grenadine
2 dashes bitters
Soda water.
Pour the first four ingredients into shaker filled with ice. Shake well. Pour into highball glass. Top off with Soda water. Garnish with lemon and orange slices.

Hot Buttered Rum
2 oz Rum
3tsp Sugar
.5tsp allspice
.5tsp cloves
1tbsp Butter
Hot Water
In a warm mug or glass add sugar and about 1.5oz of hot water and stir until sugar is dissolved. Add rum and spices and then top off with hot water. Add butter and stir until melted. Garnish with a cinnamon stick or orange peel.

Sources:

Mojito from Rum Dood http://rumdood.com/2012/06/22/mojito/ accessed 11 October 2011.

Egg Nog from Rum Dood http://rumdood.com/2009/12/08/egg-nogg accessed 11 October 2011.

Daiquiri from Rum Dood http://rumdood.com/2010/05/17/daiquiri/ accessed 11 October 2011.

Piña Colada from International Bartenders Association http://www.iba-world.com/english/cocktails/pina.php accessed 12 October 2011

Planters Punch from International Bartenders Association, http://www.iba-world.com/english/cocktails/planter php accessed 12 October 2011

Hot Buttered Rum from Rum Dood http://rumdood.com/2009/12/01/hot-buttered-rum/ accessed 11 October 2011.

Above— A panoramic view of Rumba in Seattle; below— a Rumba daquari. Photos courtesy of Rumba

Chapter 13
BEST RUM BARS IN THE WORLD

This list of bars and restaurants, while not exhaustive, is a collection of some of the best rum bars in the world. Those listed below are known for having extensive rum lists and tasty rum cocktails.

UNITED STATES

CALIFORNIA
Caña Rum Bar
714 West Olympic Blvd.
Los Angeles, CA 90014
(213)745-7090
http://213nightlife.com/canarumbar

Eva's Caribbean Kitchen
31732 Coast Hwy
Laguna Beach, CA 92651
(949) 499-6311
evascaribbeankitchen.com

Forbidden Island Tiki Lounge
1304 Lincoln Ave
Alameda, CA 94501
(510) 749-0332
info@forbiddenislandalameda.com
forbiddenislandalameda.com

Hobson's Choice
1601 Haight Street
San Francisco, CA 94117
(415) 621-5859
feedback@hobsonschoice.com
hobsonschoice.com

La Bodeguita del Medio
463 S. California Avenue
Palo Alto, CA 94306
(650) 326-7762
labodeguita.com/

La Descarga
1159 North Western Avenue
Los Angeles, CA 90039
(323) 466-1324
info@ladescargala.com
http://ladescargala.com

Smugglers Cove
630 Gough Street
San Francisco, CA 941002
(415) 869-1900
info@smugglerscovesf.com
smugglerscovesf.com

ILLINOIS
Three Dots and a Dash
435 N Clark St
Chicago, IL 60654
(312) 610-4220
http://threedotschicago.com

LOUISIANA
Cane & Table
1113 Decatur Street
New Orleans, LA 70116
(504) 581-1112

Rum House
3128 Magazine St.
New Orleans, LA
(504) 941-7560
info@rumhousenola.com
rumhousenola.com

MARYLAND
Paladar Latin Kitchen and Rum Bar
1905 Towne Center Boulevard, Suite 100
Annapolis, MD 21402
(410)897-1022
paladarkitchen.com/

NEW YORK
Cienfuegos
443 E 6th St
New York, NY 10009
(212) 614-6818
cienfuegosny.com

The Rum House
228 West 47th Steet
New York, NY 10036
(646) 490-6924
info@edisonrumhouse.com
edisonrumhouse.com

OREGON
Hale Pele Tiki Bar and Kitchen
2733 NE Broadway
Portland, OR 97232
(503) 662-8454
halepelepdx@gmail.com
http://halepele.com

PHILADELPHIA
Rum Bar
2005 Walnut Street
Philadelphia, PA 19103
(215) 751-0404
info@rum-bar.com
rum-bar.com

TEXAS
Kingston's Reggae
Fusion and Rum Bar
11342 Beechnut Street
Houston, TX 77072
(281) 495-0088
info@kingstonsrumbar.com
kingstonsrumbar.com

WASHINGTON
Rumba
1112 Pike St.
Seattle, WA 98101
(206) 583-7177
rumba@rumbaonpike.com
http://rumbaonpike.com

CANADA
Barraca, Rhumerie & Tapas
1134 Mont-Royal Est
Montreal H2J 1X8
(514) 525-7741
barraca.ca

The Reef on the Drive
1018 Commercial Drive
Vancouver, British Columbia
(604) 568-5375
thereefrestaurant@shaw.ca
thereefrestaurant.com

CARIBBEAN
La Mina Terraza
Obispo 109
Equina Oficios Plaza de Armas
Havana, Cuba 10100

Club Coconuts
Cascadia Hotel
St. Ann's
Port of Spain
Trinidad & Tobago
+868 623 6887

Skeeterz Rum Bar Grill
Main Street
Vieux Fort
St. Lucia
+758 455-1130
www.facebook.com/SkeeterzRumBarGrill

The Rum Lab
Old San Juan & Isla Verde
Puerto Rico
therumlab.com

AUSTRALIA
Cushdy
279 Hindley Street
Adelaide SA 5000
+61 8 413 721 708
cushdy.com.au

Fish D'vine
303 Shute Harbour Road
Airlie Beach Q 4802
+61 07 4948 0088
fishdvine.com.au

EUROPE

ENGLAND
Artesian
The Langham Hotel
1c Portland Place, Regent Street
London W1B 1JA
+44 020 7636 1000
info@artesian-bar.co.uk
artesian-bar.co.uk

Buena Vista Cafe & Cocktail Bar
19 Landor Road
Clapham North SW9 9R
+44 020 7326 0280
reservations@buenavistacafe.co.uk
buenavistacafe.co.uk

Cottons
70 Exmouth Market
London EC1R 4QP
+44 020 7833 3332
enquiries@cottonsislington.co.uk
cottons-restaurant.co.uk

The Redchruch Bar
107 Redchurch Street
London E2 7DL
+44 0207 739 3440
info@theredchurch.co.uk
theredchurch.co.uk

GERMANY
Rum Trader
Fasanenstraße 40
10719 Berlin
+49 30 881 1428

GREECE
Baba au Rhum
6 Kleitou Street
Athens
+30 211 7109140
info@babaaurum.com
babaaurum.com/en

ITALY
Cocktail Bar Bagno Roma
Viale Italia 49
58022 Follonica - GR
Tuscany
+39 0566 48035
cocktailbar@bagno-roma.it
barbagnoroma.it

SLOVAKIA
Rio Bratislava
Hviezdoslavovo námestie 15
Bratislava
+421 02 5441 1015
rio@riorestaurant.sk
riorestaurant.sk

SPAIN
La Compania del Ron
Maximo Aguirre Kalea, 23
48011 Bilbao, Spain
+34 94 421 3069

SWITZERLAND
Bar 63
Rolandstrasse 19
8004 Zürich
bar63.ch

Three Dots and A Dash daquari. Photographer Anjali Pinto

Chapter 14
RUM FESTIVALS

The following is a list of major rum and spirit festivals around the world that highlight and or celebrate spirits made from sugar cane. Since the specific dates and locations sometimes change from year to year, the festivals are organized roughly by the month the event usually takes place.

UNITED STATES

Miami Rum Renaissance Festival
Third week of April
Deauville Beach Resort
6701 Collins Avenue
Miami Beach, Florida 33141
http://rumrenaissance.com

Manhattan Cocktail Classic
Mid-May
New York, New York
manhattancocktailclassic.com

Atlanta Food and Wine Festival
May or June
Atlanta, Georgia
http://atlfoodandwinefestival.com

Chicago Ministry of Rum Festival
May or June
Chicago, Illinois
ministryofrum.com/events.php

Caribbean Week NYC
First week of June
New York, New York
onecaribbean.org/eventsandcalendars/
conferences

Tales of the Cocktail
Third weekend in July
New Orleans, Louisiana
talesofthecocktail.com

Indy's Whisky & Fine Spirits Expo

October
Indiana
http://eatdrinkevolve.com/events

San Francisco Cocktail Week
Mid-September
San Francisco, California
sfcocktailweek.com

Great American Distillers' Festival
October
Portland, Oregon
distillersfestival.com

OUTSIDE THE US

Barbados Food,
Wine and Rum Festival
Mid-November
Barbados
foodwinerum.com

Caribbean Week Toronto
Fourth week of October
Toronto, Canada
onecaribbean.org/eventsandcalendars/
conferences

Taste of Rum
Mid-March
San Juan, Puerto Rico
tasteofrum.com

UK Rumfest
Mid-October
London, England
http://rumfest.co.uk

Chapter 15

BIBLIOGRAPHY OF RUM

Eric Zandona

The following are a selection of books that focus on rum: its history, production and consumption. Rum has a rich, colorful and sometimes dark history that contemporary rum producers have drawn on to identify and market their products. The books listed below are a good starting point for any new rum distiller to consider when creating their product. Some of the books were not available for review but they are included below without comment for reference purposes.

HISTORIES OF RUM

HISTORIES OF RUM
DAVE BROOM; SOUTH SAN FRANCISCO: THE WINE APPRECIATION GUILD,
2003. 176 PAGES, LIST PRICE $35.00

Dave Broom is a four time Glenfiddich award winner and author of the impressive, *The World Atlas of Whisky: More than 350 Expressions Tasted — More than 150 Distilleries Explored*, editor of the *Scotch Whisky Review*, and contributor to a number of other magazines and blogs on whisky. Broom's Rum is focused on the Caribbean islands that have been at the center of rum production since its inception in the seventeenth century. While Broom draws his historical information from a number of established sources, much of the book is written from interviews of those who are intimately connected to the production of rum on each island. These interviews personalize the process of rum production and gives a human face to rum brands and distilleries that most readers will never visit. Rum emphasizes the quality of spirits being produced in the Caribbean and compares them to the finest quality Scotches and Cognacs in the World. Rum would be a great addition for any rum lover's library because it is elegantly written and has beautiful photographs by Jason Lowe. The book's one major flaw is that does not mention any of the developments of craft rum distilling reemerging in the United States.

Though this may not be completely fair considering that the book was probably researched and written before any major developments along this line. That being said, Dave Broom's Rum succeeds in enticing the reader to explore the world of high quality rums.

RUM: THE EPIC STORY OF THE DRINK
THAT CONQUERED THE WORLD.
CHARLES A. COULOMBE; NEW YORK: CITADEL, 2005. 288 PAGES,
LIST PRICE $16.99

Charles Coulombe is a writer and lecturer on a variety of topics but principally, religion and politics. He is the author of *Vicars of Christ: A History of the Popes*, and editor for the National Catholic Register. Chronologically, Rum begins with the birth of its eponymous spirit and concludes at the beginning of the twenty-first century with the fight over who invented the Mai Tai. Geographically, Coulombe's Rum travels farther afield that other histories of rum by expanding beyond the Atlantic world of the sixteenth through the nineteenth centuries and explores how rum affected the interior of Africa as well as South and Southeast Asia. The reason for Coulombe's larger geographic scope is an attempt to support his main argument, that rum was a product and catalyst of colonialism. Yet, despite this lofty goal, Coulombe fits the entire book into less than 300 pages. This is possible in part, because Coulombe relied primarily on other histories written about the triangular trade, the American Revolution, the History of West Africa, and WWI among others. Coulombe merely reinserted the story of rum where it had fallen out over time. In part because of his reliance on secondary sources, Coulombe's *Rum* gets some facts wrong and at times looses the main theme of the book. None the less, *Rum* is an interesting read which makes its most significant and interesting contribution by including a panoply of rum recipes: from historic and contemporary cocktails, to soups, stews, breads and puddings.

AND A BOTTLE OF RUM:
A HISTORY OF THE NEW WORLD IN TEN COCKTAILS.
WAYNE CURTIS; NEW YORK: THREE RIVERS PRESS, 2007. 305 PAGES,
LIST PRICE $14.95.

Wayne Curtis is a freelance writer for a number of publications including *The Atlantic*, the *New York Times*, *Men's Journal*, *American Heritage* and many others. Most of the action in Curtis' book takes place in the American Colonies, both the islands and what became the United States. The book also covers a longer time span than most of the other recent books on the history of rum. Curtis' thesis is that the story of rum is a reflection of the American people. He accomplishes this task by focusing the broad and complex history of the Americas into ten stories of popular rum cocktails and how each represented the times in which they were popular. *And a Bottle of Rum* relies heavily on secondary sources for most of its historical content which makes it very similar to other books of its type. Curtis' *And a Bottle of Rum* is an entertaining and enjoyable read though he seemed to oversimplify the complex social and economic dynamics of the Temperance Movement in the United States. His un-nuanced summary of Temperance causes me to question the rest of his historical assertions from the colonial and early Republican periods. However, one area in which *And a Bottle of Rum* stands out is in its final chapter. Curtis acknowledged and addressed the resurgence of rum in the United States and the growing interest in hand crafted spirits. Curtis' choice of format for the book, focusing on ten cocktails and the people that surrounded their creation, was a very smart way of making the history of rum interesting and approachable. And like other books in this vein, he includes a collection of colonial, classic and contemporary rum cocktail recipes for the reader.

BACARDI AND THE LONG FIGHT FOR CUBA:
THE BIOGRAPHY OF A CAUSE.
TOM GJELTEN; NEW YORK: VIKING, 2008. 480 PAGES, LIST PRICE $27.95

Tom Gjelten is an award winning writer, long-time corespondent for National Public Radio and author of *Sarajevo Daily: A City and Its Newspaper Under Siege.* Gjelten's book, *Bacardi and the Long Fight for Cuba* tracks the influence and involvement of the Bacardi family on Cuba's economic and political development over the last 150 years. Gjelten's main thesis is that, unlike any other, the story of the Bacardi family mirrors the history of Cuba from the middle of the nineteenth century onward. Gjelten was able to tell this story with the cooperation of the Bacardi family which gave him access to the personal stories and documents of their clan. Gjelten also drew from archives in Puerto Rico as well as Cuba. Bacardi and the Long Fight for Cuba is impressively documented and offers a unique lens through which to view the history of Cuba. The story of Bacardi rum, which built a family empire, is also illustrative of historical trends in the food and beverage industry that sought to develop brand name products for global markets.

CARIBBEAN RUM: A SOCIAL AND ECONOMIC HISTORY.
FREDERICK H. SMITH; GAINESVILLE: UNIVERSITY OF FLORIDA PRESS, 2008.
368 PAGES, LIST PRICE $29.95

Frederick H. Smith is an Associate Professor of Anthropology at the College of William and Mary. His research has focused on the role of Alcohol on Caribbean societies. Smith has also written *The Archeology of Alcohol and Drinking*, which looks more broadly at what archeology can tell us about drinking habits in the past than his Caribbean Rum. His first book, *Caribbean Rum*, examined the social and economic interactions that came together in the seventeenth century Atlantic world that made rum such an important spirit for the New World. One idea that resonates throughout Smith's book is that over time, rum was produced and consumed for very different historical and social reasons. Smith took an interdisciplinary approach to finding sources for *Caribbean Rum*. He used private journals, shipping ledgers, and government records as well as songs, oral tradition and archaeological evidence as the basis for the book. *Caribbean Rum* by Frederic H. Smith is the best academic examination of the lasting impact and importance of rum on the Atlantic world. Smith's thorough research creates a strong sense of credibility for his work. While *Caribbean Rum* is likely to be read only by academics and a very select group of rum enthusiasts, it will serve as a benchmark to other authors who write about the history of rum specifically and generally about the social history of drinking. *Caribbean Rum* will also serve as a great resource to future writers of the history of rum.

RUM: A SOCIAL AND SOCIABLE HISTORY OF THE REAL SPIRIT OF 1776.
IAN WILLIAMS; NEW YORK: NATION BOOKS, 2005. 368 PAGES,
LIST PRICE $16.95.

Ian Williams is a freelance writer who has written for a number of different newspapers and magazines, such as *The Nation*, and the *Financial Times*. Previous to writing *Rum*, he wrote three other books, including *Deserter: Bush's War on Military Families, Veterans and His Past*. Williams' book, *Rum*, follows the history of the cultivation of sugar cane by Europeans in the Caribbean through to the influence of rum and rum runners during national Prohibition in the United States. Williams' thesis is that rum, though quietly expunged from histories of the Americas by temperate minded writers, played a central role in the demographic, economic and political development of the region. Williams has drawn together a wide variety of sources, including a long list of scholarly works on the history of the new world, as well as primary sources from the Founding Fathers to Caribbean planters and travelers who witnessed rum production first hand. *Rum* is a well written history of the Atlantic world and it makes a strong case for how this single commodity played an important role in the development of the modern world. Because of its unique perspective Rum is a significant contribution to the historiography of the Atlantic world and it will be interesting to see how other historians respond to its methodology.

Popular Books on Rum

Arkell, Julie. *Classic Rum*. Prion, 1999. 188 pages, List Price $15.99

Ayala, Luis K. *The Rum Experience: The Complete Rum Reference*. Round Rock: Rum Runner Press Inc., 2010. 230 pages List Price $49.99.

Ayala, Luis K. and Margaret Ayala. *The Encyclopedia of Rum Drinks*. Round Rock: Rum Runner Press Inc., 2010. 232 pages, List Price $44.99

Brown, Jared McDaniel, Anistatia Renard Miller, and David Broom. *Cuba: The Legend of Rum*. London: Mixellany Books, 2009. 184 pages, List Price $21.95

Foley, Ray. *The Rum 1000: The Ultimate Collection of Rum Cocktails, Recipes, Facts, and Resources*. Naperville: Sourcebooks Inc., 2008. 320 pages, List Price $14.95

Harris, Jessica B. *Rum Drinks: 50 Caribbean Cocktails, From Cuba Libre to Rum Daisy*. San Francisco: Chronicle Books, 2010. 168 pages, List Price $19.95

Hellmich, Mittie and Frankie Frankeny. *Mini Bar: Rum: A Little Book of Big Drinks*. San Francisco: Chronicle Books, 2007. 80 pages, List Price $7.95.

Pack, James and A.J. Pack. *Nelson's Blood: The Story of Naval Rum*. Stroud: Sutton Publishing, 1995. 192 pages.

Plotkin, Robert. *Caribe Rum: The Original Guide to Caribbean Rum and Drinks*. Tucson: Barmedia, 2001. 216 pages, List Price $19.95

Chapter 14
RUM ONLINE

The websites and blogs described below are some of the most informative and well trafficked sites on the internet about rum. Contacting these sites to have your rum listed and or reviewed is a good opportunity to have your product advertised to an interested and passionate group of rum drinkers.

MINISTRY OF RUM
WWW.MINISTRYOFRUM.COM

The Ministry of Rum is a project of Edward Hamilton, rum importer and enthusiast, that has grown from a simple list of Caribbean rums to one of the most extensive rum resources on the internet. The Ministry of Rum has detailed information about each rum producing country as well as each distillery and the rums they produce. They also have a contact link for new distillers who are interested in having their rum included on the website. They also hold regular tasting events as well as tasting competitions that give out awards for the best flavored, white, dark, and premium rums.

RUM REVIEWS
WWW.RUMREVIEWS.COM

Exactly what it sounds like, Rum Reviews is a very simple and straight-forward website that reviews rums. Operated by two, self-proclaimed, amateur rum enthusiasts, they write short and clear reviews of how each rum tastes and give a rating out of 10.

RUM RUNNER PRESS
WWW.RUMRUNNERPRESS.COM

This company, lead by Luis and Margaret Ayala, operates five different websites about rum. They offer consulting services on the production and marketing of rum as well as rum education services. Their rum magazine "Got Rum?" and blog "Rum Talk" offer regular reviews of new rums on the market, as well as news affecting the rum business.

THE RUM HOWLER
HTTP://THERUMHOWLERBLOG.WORDPRESS.COM

A well trafficked blog dedicated to spirits, particularly rum and whisky. The Alberta based blogger, Chip Dykstra has reviewed a wide range of rum products and he has a dedicated email for distillers who are interested in having their rum reviewed and put on his website. Rum Howler also has an annual list for the best rums of various categories (white, dark, premium, etc.) as well as the best rums from specific regions.

RUM CONNECTION
HTTP://RUMCONNECTION.COM

This website is a source for rum news. The site creates its own original content and also acts as a news aggregator, collecting stories about rum from other sites. The creators and writers of this site like to inject a bit of humor into each of the stories they publish while also being informative.

NATIONAL RUM EXAMINER
RUMEXAMINER.COM

This news site is dedicated to rum and written by Robert Burr, author of "Rob's Rum Guide," and host of the Miami Rum Renaissance Festival. He offers regular rum reviews and stories about developments in the rum industry.

REFINED VICES
WWW.REFINEDVICES.COM

This website is dedicated to reviews and news of rum and whiskey. They also post user submitted reviews of distillery tours and interviews with distillers and master blenders. Based in Australia, they also have a dedicated link for distillers or rum blenders who would like their product reviewed and placed onto their site.

APPENDIX

Fundamentals of Distillation Glossary

Distillation is a physical process where colatile components of a liquid media are separated by virtue of their difference in boiling points (BPs). This produces a vapor significantly richer in lower-boiling-point compounds.

FUNDAMENTALS OF DISTILLATION

What is distillation?

This is a physical process where volatile components of a liquid media are separated by virtue of their difference in boiling points (BPs). This produces a vapor significantly richer in lower-boiling-point compounds. The vapor is then condensed back into a liquid with a high concentration of the lowest-boiling-point compound. The boiling of a liquid is related to a phenomenon known as vapor pressure. A liquid is made up of molecules, which travel with different velocities. For any given temperature the average velocity of all the molecules for any liquid is constant. There are a definite number however, which move faster than the average and these, which escape the surface of the liquid, exert a vapor pressure on the walls of the container. Raising the temperature of the liquid raises the energy level of the molecules, to the point where the vapor pressure equals the external pressure on the surface of the liquid. This is when the liquid reaches the boiling point. The temperature at which these pressures are equal is known as the boiling point for that particular pressure. Documented boiling points are measured at Standard Pressure (i.e. 760 mm of mercury or the air pressure at sea level).

What is vapor pressure?

Vapor pressure is the pressure exerted on the walls of a container when molecules which are moving faster than the average speed of the other molecules in a liquid escape from the surface of the liquid. Vapor pressure increases with rising temperature until at the boiling point, it equals the external pressure. In the case of two liquids in a mixture, provided the mixture is thoroughly agitated, each component exerts its own vapor pressure independent of the other. The mixture boils when the sum of the vapor pressures of the two liquids is equal to the external pressure. Because of this additive effect, the mixture boils at a temperature between the BPs of the two components. So a mixture of alcohol and water will boil at a lower temperature than the BP of water but at a higher temperature than the BP of alcohol.

What is the boiling point of alcohol vs water?

The BP of alcohol (78.4˙ Cor 173˙F) lies below that of water (100˙ C or 212˙F). These boiling points are at atmospheric pressure. A higher atmospheric pressure raises boiling points because the vapor pressure to achieve boiling has to increase to equal the external pressure. The boiling points of mixtures of alcohol and water fall between these temperatures; the higher the alcohol concentration, the closer the boiling point will be to the BP of pure alcohol.

What is batch distillation?

Batch distillation is the simplest way to increase the alcohol content of a finite amount of wash. Wash is charged into a kettle and heated to boiling. The exit vapor is passed through a pre-condenser, sometimes called a "dephlegmator," which may be internal or external. The condensate then passes through a product cooler. The alcohol content of the charge decreases as the distillation proceeds, the temperature of the charge also increases and an increasing amount of water distills together with the alcohol until there is negligible alcohol left in the pot. It usually takes two batch distillations to produce a distillate with an alcohol content of say 55% based on an 8% charge in the pot.

What are 10 lbs steam and 10 lbs steam pressure?

10 lbs of steam represents a quantity of steam, which weighs 10 lbs (i.e. which was prepared by the evaporation of 10 lbs of water). 10 lbs pressure is the pressure per square inch. At high pressures, steam will contain more heat and be at a higher temperature. It will also occupy a smaller volume than 10lbs of steam. Thus the base of a column, say at 4 pounds per square inch gauge (psig is the pressure relative to atmospheric pressure), will have a higher temperature than if it was 0 psig or 14.7 lbs absolute pressure (the air pressure at sea level).

What is the relationship between molecular weight and heat of vaporization?

The heat of vaporization of a substances is independent of its molecular weights (MW). The MW of water is 18 and its heat of vaporization is 970BTU/lb, whereas the MW of alcohol is 46 and its heat of vaporization is 356BTU/lb. So it takes less heat to vaporize a pound of alcohol than it does a pound of water. A BTU or British Thermal Unit, is the heat required to raise the temperature of 1 lb of water by 1˙F.

Why is there a difference in the quality of the distillate from a glass laboratory still and a copper pot or continuous still?

Distillation in the lab exposes the wash to a high temperature for a longer period of time than plant distillation does. Exposure to high temperatures causes elements in the wash (e.g. residual yeast or sulfur from the molasses) to decompose and vaporize with the alcohol, which ends up in the distillate. By contrast, copper stills do not tend to heat washes to the point that residual compounds vaporize and mix with the distillate. The copper also helps to eliminate sulfur from the wash; mercaptans (organic sulfur compounds), combine with the copper to form copper sulfide which precipitates out of the vapor.

Describe the distillation process in a column still.

Vapor leaving a layer of boiling liquid from one tray passes through holes or other openings in the tray above and condenses in the next liquid layer. The rising vapors condense in the liquid layer and evaporate a portion of the liquid, by a transfer of heat. The liquid flows down from tray to tray and the rising vapor exchanges part of its water molecules against an equal number of alcohol molecules, taken from the liquid. The alcohol concentration of the ascending vapor rises as it goes from tray to tray. It is interesting to note that at a given temperature between trays, the alcohol content of the vapor is higher than the alcohol content of the liquid on the tray.

What is reflux?

Reflux is a portion of the distillate vapor that re-condenses and falls back down the still. In a column still the reflux is returned to the top section of the tower to provide liquid for the upper tray. If there is no reflux, the vapor leaving the feed tray would pass via the openings in the dry upper trays and leave the tower without further increase in alcohol concentration. In the presence of reflux, the ascending vapor increases its alcohol concentration at the expense of the downward flowing liquid. At the start of feeding a column you must have total reflux to build up the alcohol inventory in the column. The reflux rate (the ratio of reflux to product) can be decreased as the alcohol inventory in the column increases. Reflux can be internal on each tray or on the top of the column if an internal dephlegmator is in place. It is external if an outside condenser is used. The product strength can also be increased in a short column (with few trays) by having a higher reflux ratio. This however requires more steam to re-vaporize the condensed liquid.

Is there a difference in composition of liquid and vapor throughout the column?

The vapor contains a higher percentage of alcohol than the liquid from which it originates. This is due to the lower boiling point of alcohol in relation to water. This is the basic principle of the distillation process. A temperature probe in the liquid phase on a tray will give the same temperature irrespective of its position between the trays. This can be seen from the temperature composition table for C_2H_5OH – water solutions, known as a McCabe-Thiele diagram which shows different alcohol compositions in the liquid and vapor for given temperatures.

Why is the top of the column cooler than the bottom?

In order for vaporization to take place in the column, the liquid must be at the boiling temperature. The percentage of alcohol and the temperature at each point in the column are interdependent. Thus the higher the alcohol content the lower the boiling point. Alcohol content increases as the vapor rises up the column so the top is cooler than the bottom of the column.

What three controlled factors determine the alcohol concentration in the distillate?

Feed rate: The higher the feed rate the greater the quantity of alcohol that can be picked up by the ascending vapor in the tower.

Rate of reflux/product flow. Both are independent. A change in reflux rate affects the concentration of alcohol on the trays. Since the alcohol content of the ascending vapor depends on the alcohol content of the liquid on the trays, you can regulate the concentration of the distillate by regulating the reflux rate.

An increase in steam flow leads to a decrease in the alcohol concentration in the distillate. This is due to the excess water produced when the steam condenses.

How does liquid travel in a tower?

The liquid flows through down pipes (downcomers) from one tray to the next. The lower end of each downcomer is inserted into a cup which acts as a liquid trap so that vapor cannot go up the downcomers. This also allows the liquid to flow evenly across the trays. In some modern columns there are no downcomers on the trays. These are called "dual flow trays" where the liquid and vapor both pass through the holes on the tray. The turn-down ratio on these columns is limited; steam pressure and input must be carefully balanced with the liquid flow.

Up to what height does the liquid fill each tray in a column?

The liquid height on a tray will be slightly above the height of the outlet weir. If the tray is dual flow, the height will be dependent on the steam pressure holding up the liquid on the tray. These work well with columns that are operated under pressure. It is the head on each tray that creates the base pressure in the column.

Describe the bubble cap and its function

The bubble caps consist of inverted cups fitted over small vapor pipes or chimneys. The vapor from the tray below traveling up the chimney hits the top of the inverted cup and spreads through the liquid via small slots in the bottom of the cup. This breaks the vapor into small bubbles thereby making better contact with the liquid. There are several methods of doing this; bubble caps are just one device.

Why is there a difference in pressure between the bottom and top of the column?

In order to cause vapor to flow up the column, there must be a pressure differential between the bottom and the top. The greater the pressure applied at the base, the larger the quantity of vapor that will travel through the column, thus the rate of operation will affect the pressure differential and vapor velocity.

As the vapor travels through the column it must pass through layers of liquid on each tray. This static head represents the pressure, which is required to force the vapor through these liquid layers. The combined weight of the liquid layers contributes to the total pressure at the base of the column.

In a batch rectification system, the number of trays in the column is limited because of the lower vapor pressure leaving the pot. Product taken from the condenser/cooler has limited separation of congeners in a short column so heads, hearts, and tails must be carefully selected using organoleptic means. The distinction between the three is not that clear.

Why must a distillation with sieve trays be operated within a certain range?

The velocity of the upward vapor must be sufficient to prevent liquid from falling through the perforations. If the steam flow is reduced to such an extent that the liquid begins to pass through the holes the contact between ascending vapor and descending beer is lessened and not all the alcohol will be vaporized. If the beer flow is lessened but not the steam, the distillate strength will reduce because of the excess water introduced in the form of steam. Feed and steam must be balanced.

What can occur if a column is operated above capacity?
Overloading the column with feed would result in a high vapor velocity. This will in turn increase the pressure differential between the bottom and top of the column. The excessive pressure and velocity of the vapor reduces vapor to liquid contact on the trays; this can result in carry-over of liquid from tray to tray (entrainment).

If a still is operated above its capacity, the high pressure interferes with the flow of liquid through the downcomers and the column will flood.
This is why the diameter of the column, the size of the downcomers, and the size of the holes must be carefully calculated to handle the designed flow through the column. The spacing between trays is also important to prevent entrainment (pulling one liquid along with another). Spacing is higher in a beer column to allow for cleaning and foaming; it is less in the rectifier since the alcohol does not foam. Perforations in a beer column take up about 5 – 7 % of the total tray area.

What is the boiling point of fusel oil in comparison to water and what are the boiling points of fusel oil mixtures?
The boiling point of fusel oil is about 130°C or 270°F, which is higher than water. The mixture boils at a lower temperature than does either component. In contrast to miscible liquids, alcohol and water, the boiling point of a mixture of two immiscible liquids (liquids incapable of mixing) is constant, that is, independent of the concentration of two components. For this reason, fusel oil, i.e. the mixture of fusel oils (containing some alcohol), accumulates at the same temperature regardless of concentration. This is important in controlling the rectifier by the mid-column temperature controller. The thermometer is installed in an area where a small change in alcohol concentration has the greatest effect on temperature, namely the fusel oil zone. The other method of controlling product flow and strength is a density meter installed on the

product line which regulates the product flow valve.

Why does fusel oil block a column?

Fusel oil accumulates in the lower third of the column depending on the quality of spirit desired and the feed location. If not removed it eventually begins to blanket the liquid layer on the tray. A mixture of fusel oil and water boils at a temperature below the boiling point of either component, i.e., less than 100°C, 212°F provided the molecules of both materials have access to the surface and the opportunity to escape. As soon as the liquid on the tray separates into two layers, the bottom layer of water continues to boil, however its molecules condense in the fusel oil layer rather than evaporate. Because of its high boiling point, the fusel oil layer does not give off sufficient vapor to maintain the distillation in the upper part of the column. The accumulation of fusel oil manifests itself in a reduced output of distillate in spite of adding more steam to the base of the column. This in turn will increase the base pressure in the column. A layer of fusel oil on the tray is desirable but this should not be excessive. The layer is the most stable point in the column, hence it is the best location for controlling the flow of product from the column, if a density meter is not selected.

Why is the location of the proper draw for fusel oil affected by the concentration of alcohol in the column?

The boiling point of a mixture of two immiscible liquids (e.g. fusel oil and water) is independent of the concentration of two components. The mixture of fusel oil, water, and some alcohol in the column accumulates at the same temperature regardless of the oil concentration. The temperature of liquid on each tray depends on the alcohol concentration. Fusel oil accumulates on a tray which corresponds in temperature (and therefore in alcohol concentrations) to the constant boiling point of the oil/water/alcohol mixture. The location of the oil draw is independent of the oil concentration but depends on the alcohol concentration in the column. An increase in alcohol forces the oil down; the opposite occurs when the alcohol content decreases. This is the principle of maintaining equilibrium in the column where the mid-column temperature is maintained at about 185°F or 85°C and the strength on the plate is at about 75% alcohol.

What are the major constituents of fusel oil?

About 75% amyl alcohols, 20% butyl alcohols, and 5% other alcohols. Excess water and alcohol can be removed from fusel oil by salting out with a saturated salt solution in the storage tank. The oil will float and the water/alcohol can be drawn from the bottom. Fusel oils originate from amino acids, which are formed by the hydrolysis of proteins present in the wash/beer and to some extent from the protein in the yeast cell. Isopropyl and n-butyl alcohols have been traced to the action of butyric acid bacteria on the sugar in the substrate. This is the bacteria responsible for creating esters in high ester rums, the ester being butyl acetate.

Fusel oil formation can be caused by the following: Nitrogen poor yeast and the form in which nitrogen is provided can produce more or less fusel oil. The optimum temperature of the yeast strain must be known. A yeast strain fermented at the wrong temperature can create an excess of congeners. Fusel oil formation increases with longer fermentation times but it reaches a maximum concentration and remains constant thereafter; fusel oil formation at a 0.4% level can inhibit fermentation and it is toxic to yeast above 0.7%.

A longer time interval between fermentation and distillation tends to increase the amount of fatty acids (aliphatic alcohols) formed. Again wash/beer is not a good practice if fatty acids are not desirable. Acrolein (pepper spirit) can also be formed if there is secondary fermentation or if one ferments on a falling temperature.

What operational factor determines the separation of heads and product collected from the beer or rectifying columns?

The concentration of heads in the distillate is regulated by the manner in which the vent condenser is operated to separate low boilers from the reflux. In a pot or batch rectifying still, it is selected organoleptically.

What is an azeotrope?

It is the composition at which two compounds cannot be separated by simple distillation. Water and alcohol form an azeotrope at 95.63% alcohol and 4.37% water. At this point, the liquid boils at 172.76°F, 78.2°C which is lower than the boiling points for ethanol (173.12°F, 78.4°C) and water (212°F, 100°C). To achieve higher concentrations of alcohol, a third liquid, usually benzene, is added to the mixture which breaks the azeotrope and allows higher rectification. However, the resulting liquid must be processed again to remove the benzene.

Why can high condenser temperatures increase alcohol losses?

Incondensable gases expand and the resultant high vapor velocity leads to entrainment of alcohol droplets through the vent line to the condenser. A high temperature will also increase the solubility of alcohol in the incondensable gases. A final condenser must always be vented to allow for the escape of incondensable gases from the distillation system.

Name three types of heat exchangers.

Shell-and-tube, where the vapors pass through the tubes and the cooling medium circulates around the tubes causing the vapors to condense.

Plate-and-frame, where rectangular grooved trays are sandwiched together on a supporting frame. This is usually used to exchange heat between liquids rather than a vapor and a liquid.

Coil type, where there is a pipe in a tank of coolant or water. The vapor to be condensed and cooled passes through the coil, the surrounding fluid acts as the coolant.

Describe a condenser and its function.

A condenser was originally a tightly wound coil in a tank of flowing water. Today it can be a bundle of tubes in a shell. The vapor from the still passes through the tubes while cold water passes through the shell side. This is important in the case of muddy water since it would be impossible to clean the inside of the tubes if the arrangement was reversed. Condensers can be arranged in more than one pass where the water makes several passes through the tubes. Condensers are usually vented, unless there is more than one condenser in the system. The first condenser is sometimes referred to as a dephlegmator. In a beer still it is usually the beer preheater.

The last (vent) condenser, which is vented to atmosphere, allows the passage of incondensable gases (air or carbon dioxide) that would otherwise create a back pressure in the column. The vent also permits equalization of pressure thereby permitting a free flow of liquid from the condenser. It is allowed to puff by keeping it warm and a heads fraction is usually taken from it. Cooling water is controlled by the temperature in the shell or this thermometer may be connected to a control valve that directs vapor from the main condenser to the vent condenser.

Why the oversized discharge leg from the condenser and why is there a "U" on the pipe that returns liquid to the column?

This allows for a free flow of liquid back to the column and space for incondensable gases to escape. The "U" in the reflux line provides a seal between the column and the condenser outlet thereby preventing vapor from leaving the tower.

What prevents steam from escaping through the outlet pipe of the column?

The liquid level that must be maintained in the base of the column, say about 18" to 24". This level is maintained by a float device or level controller, which modulates the outlet valve. Failure to maintain a proper level will result in steam (energy) wasted through the outlet valve.

What is the importance of a waste tester in the base of the column?

The waste tester, to detect any alcohol in the base of the column, takes vapor from about plate 8, condenses and cools it prior to testing. Since it is the alcohol in the vapor that is being measured there may be some alcohol that may not be in the liquid leaving the still. Remember that the vapor has more alcohol than the liquid from which it was vaporized.

Testing the effluent is not good since the alcohol, if any, will flash as soon as the stream hits the atmosphere. It is important to inject saturated steam into a column; superheated steam can distort temperature values at the base of the column and bake the calcium, in the case of fermented molasses, on the tray surfaces.

Why is the finished product taken from the upper trays in the column?

Acetaldehyde and other highly volatile components accumulate in the top of the column. They go as vapor to the condensers and are withdrawn from the condensate of the vent condenser. The product is withdrawn as a liquid from one of the upper trays.

Why does high-strength distillate require more steam than low strength distillate?

The former requires a higher reflux rate so more energy is needed to vaporize the liquids. That is, there must be more vapor going to the condenser to create more reflux. If more steam is used for the low proof distillate it is because the still is poorly designed or operated. The steam reappears as excess water in the distillate. Rectifying columns with say 60 trays will require a lower reflux ratio, hence less steam to produce a higher strength, cleaner product.

Why does an efficient still, in relation to fractionation, use less steam than an inefficient still?

The efficiency of a column depends on the contact between liquid and vapor. In an inefficient still the vapor doesn't get to transfer its heat of vaporization to the liquid on the tray. The vapor leaving the top of the column therefore contains excess water. In order to obtain a high-strength product you must use a higher reflux ratio and therefore more steam. Bubble caps are probably the most efficient practical way of transferring heat to the liquid on a tray. The column must have enough trays to produce a strong distillate and effective fractionation of the congeners. The diameter is related to the volume of vapor that must pass up the column. Sieve trays are cheaper than bubble cap or tunnel trays. They are used mainly in the beer column for easy cleaning. Packed columns are not recommended since the vapor and liquid tend to channel and the packing tends to adsorb impurities. Taking a side draw from a packed column is impossible so they are only used occasionally in batch systems.

What is the relationship between column diameter and capacity?

A column of 6 foot diameter handles 9 times as much liquid as a 2 foot diameter still. The capacity is proportional to the square of the diameter. Bear in mind that the downcomers must handle the flow of liquid and the holes or other uprising devices (tunnels or bubble caps etc) must handle the vapor load.

When a rectifying column is being boiled out, a distillate of low alcohol concentration and inferior quality is collected, why?

In boiling out the column, the quantity of alcohol decreases and fusel oil becoming immiscible in the upper part is distilled over with the product. This is also the principle behind extractive distillation or hydro-selection, a term seldom used.

How is fractionation efficiency affected by vapor velocity and liquid flow?

An increase in vapor velocity reduces the fractionation efficiency because of entrainment. Low vapor velocity reduces the chance of entrainment and increases tray efficiency. This is because the interaction between liquid droplets and vapor in the space between trays is intimate and the liquid does not get carried to the next tray. The rate of liquid flow, on the other hand has little effect on tray efficiency.

How to prevent a vacuum in a column or pot still.

During start up, open steam is used to heat up the column or pot. If cold feed is introduced the vapor in the column will quickly condense thus causing an instant vacuum. Columns are not normally designed to withstand vacuum. The vacuum breaker on any still should be ample in diameter to allow lots of air to enter the column. It is important to get a column hot before introducing the feed. The beer heater should warm the feed sufficiently to prevent the phenomenon of cold feed entering the column.

How to measure efficiency and losses expected on a system.

Efficiency is a measure of the recovery rate and should be calculated as the ethanol in product divided by the ethanol in the feed, expressed as a percentage. There is also an operating efficiency, which is the production achieved divided by design capacity expressed as a percentage. Another indicator is the energy efficiency, which is the net energy input divided by the volume of alcohol recovered. The total losses in various streams from a system will be:

Stillage	0.3%
Fusel Oil	0.3%
Vents	0.2%
Heads, if dumped	1.5%
Total loss potential	2.3%

So the optimum efficiency of an alcohol system should be about 97.7%. This loss will be exceeded if poor steam conditions prevail or if insufficient cooling water is applied. There must be a liquid seal at the bottom of each column (a liquid level is maintained about the outlet) and condensers should be clean and efficient. A small amount of vapor is allowed to puff through the vents to cause incondensable gases and very light boilers (e.g. methanol) to escape.

This does not apply to the second distillate on a pot where heads and tails fractions may be as high as 5% and 20% respectively. In this case the tails and maybe some of the heads fraction can be returned to the wash/beer charge in the primary distillation. These are not hard and fast rules, the percentages must be determined by the character of the final distillate and the desires of the distiller.

GLOSSARY

Adams pot still: A pot still with two retorts, commonly used in Jamaica.

Aerobic: Biological activity that takes place in the presence of oxygen. Many metabolic functions, as well as yeast propagation, require oxygen to be carried out.

Agitator: A motorized paddle that stirs the contents inside a pot still to prevent solids from sticking to the sides and burning.

Aguardiente: An early name for cane distillates made in Spanish speaking territories.

Alcohol by volume: A measurement of the alcohol content of a liquid per unit of volume.

Alcohol by weight: A measurement of the weight of the alcohol as a percentage of the total mass of the liquid.

Aldehydes: Organic compounds that are produced by the removal of hydrogen from alcohols (oxidation) and tend to be highly aromatic and detectable at lower concentrations than alcohols. It is also thought that the oxidation in the body contributes to hangovers and headaches.

Anaerobic: Biological activity that takes place in a low oxygen or oxygen-free environment. Some bacteria and yeast strains ferment anaerobically.

Analyzer: The first column of a continuous still, the analyzer vaporizes alcohol with rising steam as wash descends through a series of trays.

Anti-foam: An agent that can be added to the still during the first run to prevent or reduce the size of the foam cap on top of the wash. These agents work by reducing the surface tension of the liquid and help prevent foam getting stuck to hard to clean areas of the still.

Ash: Non-sugar solids found in molasses. Ash can be made up of dirt, mineral matter, and or sulfur dioxide.

Azeotrope: Is a mixture of two liquids that cannot be separated by simple distillation. Alcohol and water form an azeotrope at 95.63% ethanol and 4.37% water by weight and boils at 78.2°C, 172.8 °F.

Beer still: A name for a pot still used for stripping runs in whiskey distilleries.

Blending: Mixing two or more distillates, of different bases or from different producers, to create a new flavor profile.

Bottle shock: After bottling wine and spirits the flavors and aromas can become muted and unbalanced. The pre-bottling profile tends to return after a few weeks.

Brix: A measurement of the percentage of sugar in a given solution

Bubb tun: The last tank in the series of yeast starters before the yeast culture is introduced to the main fermentation vessel.

Bubble caps: They serve as additional surfaces inside of a column still on which vapors can condense and re-vaporize. This process helps to refine the spirit as the vapors rise from one plate to the next.

Bung: A stopper often made of oak that plugs the hole in the side of a barrel.

Cane solids: The non-sugar particles found in sugar cane juice and molasses that contribute to the flavor of the distillate. Cane solids consist of minerals, soil, and ash.

Charge: The fermented wash put into a pot still.

Colandria: A steam powered heat exchanger inside a wort boiler or pot still that heats the surrounding liquid.

Condenser: Cools vapors into liquid by transferring heat from the vapor to a cool liquid surrounding the piping.

Congeners: Organic chemical compounds like aldehydes, polyphenols and aromatic esters, created during fermentation and contribute flavors and aromas.

Dead wash: A low abv alcohol solution that has fully fermented out and no longer contains live yeast.

Dephlegmator: Also known as a pre-condenser, it is used to control the amount of reflux in a still. By adjusting the coolant flow rate running through the coils a distiller can increase or decrease the amount of reflux at the top of the still and better control the composition of the vapor leaving the still.

Diammonium phosphate (DAP): A water soluble salt that is used as a yeast nutrient by providing much needed nitrogen and it also affects the pH of the mash.

Dunder: Dunder is the spent liquid left in the still after the rum wash has undergone the stripping run.

Ebulliometer: A device used to measure the boiling point of a liquid. Since alcohol boils at a lower temperature than water (78.4°C vs 100°C) the alcohol content of a liquid can be measured within +/-0.5% abv by determining its boiling point.

Esters: A group of chemical compounds that form by condensing an acid with an alcohol during fermentation or distillation. Esters with low molecular weight are aromatic and produce floral or fruity smells such as apple, banana, pears, pineapple, and strawberry.

Feints: A term used for the last fraction of the distillate, also known as the tails.

Fermenter: A biological agent that carries out the work of fermentation.

Fermentor: A vessel or container in which fermentation takes place.

Ferti-irrigation: A process of simultaneously fertilizing and irrigating crops with a nutrient rich liquid.

Fractionation efficiency: A measure of the amount of heat and time applied to the wash or low wines before alcohol begins to separate.

Fusel oils: Also known as fusel alcohols, they are higher order alcohols formed during fermentation at high temperatures, low pH, or when yeast activity is limited by a lack of nitrogen. They have an oily consistency are concentrated at the end of distillation or in the tails. Very high concentrations can produce off flavors or taste hot.

Heads: The first distillate to come off the still comprised largely of methanol, aldehydes and ethanol. They can be discarded or collected and added to the tails for re-distillation.

Hearts: The middle fraction of a distillation run which is comprised mostly of ethanol and some congeners. The hearts are the potable spirit that becomes rum, brandy, whiskey, etc.

High wines: In rum parlance, high wines are the first half of the tails, and are used to fill the second retort of an Adam's still for a future run. High wines are typically about 75% abv. Generally, high wines refers to as a mixed spirit made from adding the low wines and some portion of the heads and/or tails from a previous spirit run before a second distillation.

Hydrolysis: A chemical reaction in which water reacts with a compound to produce other compounds. It involves the splitting of the ether linkage chemical bond and the addition of the hydrogen cation and the hydroxide anion from water.

Hydrometers: A tool that measures the density of one liquid relative to the density of a second. Hydrometers can be calibrated to measure: specific gravity, density, percent alcohol, percent radiator glycol, percent sugar and brix among others.

Immiscible liquids: Liquids that are incapable of mixing.

Inoculum: A mixture of yeast with a sugar solution designed to grow a yeast colony to sufficient size that the yeast does not become over stressed in a large fermentation vessel.

Kill-devil: An early English name for rum.

Krebs cycle: A series of chemical reactions used by aerobic organisms to generate energy.

Live wash: A mash that is actively being fermenting by live yeast.

Low wines: In rum parlance, low wines are the second half of the tails, and are used to fill the first retort of an Adam's still for a future run. Low wines are typically about 35% abv. Generally, low wines refers to a low proof spirit created during the first distillation of a wash.

Lyne Arm: The pipe or tubing running from the top of the still to the condenser. The height, diameter and angle of the lyne arm all contribute to the character of the spirit produced by the still. Generally a down angle will allow more flavor elements in the wash or low wines to come through where as a 90° angle will allow a little less and an up angle greater than 90° will allow less of the congeners to pass into the condenser.

Marry: When blended or vatted spirits are allowed to sit together and mix before bottling.

Mashing: Creating a sugar solution that is within the proper parameters for fermentation.

Maturation: A series of chemical reactions and interactions between a spirit and oak that affects the color, flavor and mouthfeel. The rate at which maturation takes place is dependent on a number of factors, including: temperature, humidity, pressure and the ratio of oak surface area to volume of spirit.

Molasses Spirit: A neutral spirit made from molasses that has been highly rectified, similar to neutral grain spirits.

Nose: Can refer either to the aroma of a given spirit or the act of smelling to determine its aromatic characteristic.

Ogee: A small bulb-like shaped bulge typically just above the pot still in the neck

Organoleptic: The visual, aromatic, flavor and mouthfeel sensations created by a libation.

pH: (from potential of Hydrogen) A measure of the hydrogen-ion concentration in a solution. The scale ranges from 0 to 14 of the acidity or alkalinity of a solution where less than 7 is more acidic, 7 is neutral and greater than 7 is more alkaline.

Pitching: The process of mixing yeast into a mash to begin the process of fermentation.

Preheater: A device to heat up the wash before it enters a column still.

Proof: In the US proof is a measurement defined as twice the percentage of alcohol by volume.

Receiver: A container in which low wines or spirits can flow into during distillation.

Rectifier: A column attached to a still that contains plates or bubble caps. A rectifier increases the amount of separation in a run compared to a simple pot still.

Reflux: A process in which distillate vapors re-condense to be re-vaporized.

Retort: A device that contains a liquid of various alcohol concentration like low or high wines. As vapors pass through the retort the alcohol concentration of the vapors increase. The name "retort" is almost exclusively used in the context of making rum while in other contexts, such as whiskey making, it is often called a "thumper" or "thump keg."

Scaling: Mineral buildup on the interior surface of a still.

Separation: In the context of distillation, separation refers to how well ethanol is separating from components in the wash like congeners, fusel oils and water.

Solera: A system of fractional blending where only some portion of a barrel (usually one-third to one-half) that has matured the longest is bottled and a slightly younger spirit is used to refill the barrel.

Specific gravity: The density of a substance relative to the density of water, usually measured with a hydrometer.

Spirit run: The final distillation run to produce a new make spirit that can either be bottled or matured with oak.

Steam jacket: A device used for heating the contents of a pot still. The jacket usually covers the bottom two-thirds of the pot and hot steam fills the space between the still wall and the jacket wall, heating the contents.

Sterilization: The process of making an object free of live bacteria or other microorganisms. In a distillery, complete sterilization is almost impossible to achieve even with proper sanitation practices.

Stripping run: The first distillation of a fermented wash meant to concentrate the alcohol content. The resulting distillate is often referred to as "low wines" and serves as the input for a subsequent spirit run.

Sugars: A class of chemically related, sweet tasting carbohydrates. Sucrose is most abundant in sugar cane and sugar beets. Maltose is a sugar created by the breakdown of grain starches by the amylase enzyme. In rum production, only sucrose obtained from sugar cane is allowed.

Tails: The spirits coming off of the still at the end of a run. Generally, spirits with lower alcohol strength have higher concentrations of both positive congeners and undesirable impurities (i.e tails).

Thermophilic: A characteristic of some organisms that live and thrive in high temperature environments, often between 113°F and 252°F (45-122 °C).

Thermostatic control valve: A temperature-controlled valve that can be calibrated to allow spirit vapors to pass to the condenser only after it has reached the set temperature.

Vatting: Mixing two or more distillates of the same base from the same producer to create a new flavor profile.

Viscosity: The resistance of a fluid to flow or deform. Viscosity is caused by friction between the moving particles in a liquid. Molasses is more viscous than sugar cane juice.

Wine thief: A pipette anywhere from 12" to 24" in length for removing a small sample of spirits from a barrel. Wine thieves can be made from glass, stainless-steel or food grade plastic but acrylic should never be used with spirits.

INDEX

A

aging. *See maturation*
agitator 76, 137
aguardiente 6, 9, 137
alchemists 6
aldehydes 8, 61, 70–72
American Distilling Institute xi, 15
American Revolution xii, 112
Angostura 10–11
Antigua 9
Appleton x, 98
atmospheric pressure 81–82, 124

B

Bacardi 10, 96, 113
Barbados 6, 8, 95, 109
barrels xiii, 15, 17, 19–21, 24, 27, 32, 38–39, 81–82, 85, 89, 98–100
batch distillation xii, 73–80, 124
Belize 9
blend(ing) 11–12, 15, 20–21, 23, 25, 32, 44–45, 48, 51, 62, 67, 71, 74, 83–85, 89–90, 98–100, 138, 141–142
bottle shock 90, 138
bottling 20, 25, 32, 84, 89–90
brandy 6, 8, 9, 19, 37–38, 67–69, 86
Brandy 102
Brazil 11–12, 43
Broom, David 111–112, 115
bubble cap 70, 76, 78, 127, 133, 138, 141
burnt sugar. *See spirit caramel*

C

cachaça 12, 43
California 98, 105, 109
Canada x–xi, 7, 9, 11, 29, 83, 106, 109
Canary Islands 5
cane fields 5, 97

Captain Morgan 5, 95, 97
caramel. *See spirit caramel*
Caribbean x–xi, 6, 8, 10, 13, 26, 62, 74–76, 97–98, 105, 106, 109, 111
Charles A. Coulombe 112
Christian Carl 27, 29
Citadelle Gin 99
cocktails 6, 101, 101–103, 105, 112, 113
Coffey still 9, 69–71
Cognac Ferrand 99
Columbus 5
column still 10
condenser 17–18, 23, 31, 38, 68–71, 74–80, 125, 127, 130–132, 134, 138, 140–141, 143
Cruzan 10, 99
Cuba 6–7, 10, 95, 101, 106, 113, 115
Curtis, Wayne 112–113

D

dark and stormy 20
diammonium phosphate 51, 54, 58, 63, 85–86, 139
Dominica 9
Dominican Republic 95
Don Q 98
dunder 9–10, 23, 60–61, 63, 70–72, 85–86, 139

E

eau-de-vie de molasses 6
England 6, 95, 107, 109
esters 49, 55, 59, 61, 70–73, 81, 97, 130, 139

F

feints 24, 29, 87–88, 139
fermentation xii, 8, 12, 17, 23, 29, 57–66, 130; *efficiency* 57, 65–66; *temperature* 17, 23, 29, 37, 53, 59–60, 64, 78
fermentor 17, 37, 46, 47, 49, 57–61, 63–66, 85–86, 139
fertilizer 5–6, 51, 54

filtering 20, 25, 29, 32
Flor de Caña 96
France 9, 95, 99
fusel alcohol 72, 139
fusel oil 47, 61, 70–72, 128–130, 133–134, 142

G

Germany 23, 29, 83, 107
gin 6–7, 21, 68, 71, 99
Gjelten, Tom 113
glycol 76, 78, 140
Grenada 9, 99
Guadeloupe 9, 95, 97
Guatemala 9
Guyana 8–9, 95

H

Haiti 6, 9
Havana Club 10
heads 12, 18–19, 24–25, 31–32, 68, 70, 75, 80, 87–88, 127, 130–131, 134, 139
hearts 18–19, 24, 29, 31, 68, 75, 80, 87–88, 140
Hillrock Estate Distillery 100
Hispaniola 5
Holstein 21, 23
humidity 81–82, 141

I

India 5, 11, 41

J

Jamaica x, 6–8, 61–65, 67, 83, 95, 99, 137
Japan 7

K

Kentucky 17
kill-devil 6

L

low wines 18, 73, 75, 87–88, 140

M

Martinique 95, 97, 98
mashing 53–56, 141
Massachusetts xii, 13, 21
maturation xi–xiii, 15,

19–20, 24, 32, 38–39, 81–83, 88–89, 98–100, 141

Mauritius 11

Mexico 10–11

Ministry of Rum 15, 109, 117

molasses xii–xiii, 5–12, 15, 17–18, 21, 23, 25–32, 41–54; *blackstrap* 10, 25–27, 43–44, 62, 85; *early uses* 5; *pretreatment* 46, 53–56

muscovado 5

N

Neisson Rhum 98

Nepal 11

New England xii, 13, 15, 25

Newport Distilling Company 25–32

New World 5, 112, 114–115

Nicaragua 9, 95

nutrients xiii, 17, 21, 45, 47, 49, 50–51, 53, 60, 72

O

oxygen demand 72

P

Panama 9

Philippines 5

Plantation Rum 99

pot still 8–10, 17, 21, 23, 25–27, 29, 37–38, 43, 61, 67–69, 72–80, 85–87, 95, 141, 142; *Adams pot still* 61, 67, 137

prohibition 114

Prohibition 7, 13, 95

proofing 20, 25, 32

Puerto Rico 6, 10–11, 95, 106, 109, 113

R

rectification column 73–80

reflux 24, 31, 68, 70, 74, 76, 78, 125–126, 130, 132–133, 139, 142

retort 17–19, 38, 67–68, 137, 140, 142

Rhode Island xii, 25–27

Rhum J.M. 98

Ron Zacapa 100

rum bars 105–107

rum books 111–116

rum festivals 109

Rum Runner Press 117

rums online 117–118

rum styles 95–100; *amber rum* xiii, 10, 15, 21, 85; *black rum* 20, 25, 96–97; *dark rum* xiii, 6, 27, 101–103; *Demerara* 8; *full-bodied* 83, 95–97; *light* 7, 70, 101–102; *medium-bodied* 7, 9, 61–62, 67, 95–96, 98; *Navy rum* 9; *rum agricole* 9, 95–98; *rumbullion* 6–7; *single barrel* 17, 19, 26–27, 32, 99; *single vintage* 99; *spiced rum* 15, 95, 97; *verschnitt* 62; *white rum* xiii, 7, 15, 20, 82, 96, 101

Ryan & Wood Distillery 21–25

S

Sailor Jerry 97

Scotland xi, 7, 82

slavery 5, 41

Solera 82, 100, 142

Southwest Asia 5

Spain 5–6, 11, 107

spirit caramel xiii, 6, 8–10, 20, 25, 41, 51–52, 85, 89–90, 97

spirit run 18–19, 27, 31, 75, 87–88, 140, 142

St. Croix 10–11

steam jacket 76, 142

St. George Spirits 98

stripping run 18, 27, 29, 32, 75, 87–88, 138–139, 142

sugar cane 5–6, 12, 41–45, 97–98; *cultivation* 41–44; *processing* 5–6, 44–47

sugar crystals 5, 42

Surinam 9

T

tails 18–19, 24, 31–32, 68, 75, 87–88, 127, 134, 142

totes 37

Trinidad 10, 95, 99, 106

Turkey Shore Rum Distillery 13–20

V

vatting 20, 25, 32, 67, 83–84, 143

Vendome Copper & Brass Works 17

vodka xi, 7, 21, 48, 71, 97

W

water chemistry 46

West Indies 5, 9, 42, 82, 83, 97

whiskey x–xi, 19, 26, 37–39, 46–47, 85–86, 98–100, 118, 138, 140

Williams, Ian 114–115

wine xiv, 38, 47, 55, 57, 89–90, 100, 109, 138; *prune* 8; *sherry* 8, 100

Y

yeast xiii–xiv, 8–10, 12, 15, 27, 29, 37, 41, 43, 45–50, 54–55, 57–65, 70, 72, 85–86, 130, 137–141; *effect on flavor* 49, 61, 72, 98; *nutrition* 17, 21, 23, 46, 50–51, 63, 86; *propagation* xi, 57–59